Collins

The Shangl Maths Project

For the English National Curriculum

Series Editor: Professor Lianghuo Fan

UK Curriculum Consultant: Paul Broadbent

Practice Book  1

William Collins' dream of knowledge for all began with the publication of his first book in 1819. A self-educated mill worker, he not only enriched millions of lives, but also founded a flourishing publishing house. Today, staying true to this spirit, Collins books are packed with inspiration, innovation and practical expertise. They place you at the centre of a world of possibility and give you exactly what you need to explore it.

Collins. Freedom to teach.

Published by Collins
An imprint of HarperCollins*Publishers* Ltd.
The News Building
1 London Bridge Street
London SE 1 9GF

Browse the complete Collins catalogue at
www. collins. co. uk

© HarperCollins*Publishers* Limited 2015
© Professor Lianghuo Fan 2015
© East China Normal University Press Ltd. 2015

10 9 8 7 6 5 4 3 2 1

ISBN: 978-0-00-814462-3

The Shanghai Maths Project (for the English National Curriculum) is a collaborative effort between HarperCollins, East China Normal University Press Ltd. and Professor Lianghuo Fan and his team. Based on the latest edition of the award-wining series of learning resource books, *One Lesson One Exercise*, by East China Normal University Press Ltd. in Chinese, the series of Practice Books is published by HarperCollins after adaptation following the English National Curriculum.

Practice book Year 1 is translated and developed by Professor Lianghuo Fan with assistance of Ellen Chen, Ming Ni, Huiping Xu and Dr. Lionel Pereira-Mendoza, with Paul Broadbent as UK curriculum consultant.

British Library Cataloguing in Publication Data
A Catalogue record for this publication is available from the British Library.

Series Editor: Professor Lianghuo Fan
UK Curriculum Consultant: Paul Broadbent
Commissioned by Lee Newman
Project Managed by Fiona McGlade and Mike Appleton
Design by Kevin Robbins and East China Normal University Press Ltd.
Typesetting by East China Normal University Press Ltd.
Cover illustration by Daniela Geremia
Production by Rachel Weaver
Printed by Grafica Veneta S. p. A.

Contents

Chapter 1　Numbers up to 10

1.1　Let's begin / 1

1.2　Let's sort (1) / 3

1.3　Let's sort (2) / 5

1.4　Let's count (1) / 7

1.5　Let's count (2) / 9

1.6　Let's count (3) / 11

1.7　Let's count (4) / 13

1.8　Let's count (5) / 15

1.9　Let's count (6) / 17

1.10　Counting and ordering
numbers (1) / 19

1.11　Counting and ordering
numbers (2) / 21

1.12　Let's compare (1) / 23

1.13　Let's compare (2) / 25

1.14　The number line / 27

Unit test 1 / 29

**Chapter 2　Addition and subtraction
within 10**

2.1　Number bonds / 33

2.2　Addition (1) / 35

2.3　Addition (2) / 37

2.4　Addition (3) / 39

2.5　Let's talk and calculate (I) / 41

2.6　Subtraction (1) / 43

2.7　Subtraction (2) / 45

2.8　Subtraction (3) / 47

2.9　Let's talk and calculate (II) / 49

2.10　Addition and subtraction / 51

2.11　Addition and subtraction
using a number line / 53

2.12　Games of number 10 / 55

2.13　Adding three numbers / 57

2.14　Subtracting three numbers / 59

2.15　Mixed addition and
subtraction / 61

Unit test 2 / 63

**Chapter 3　Numbers up to 20 and
their addition and subtraction**

3.1　Numbers 11 – 20 / 65

3.2　Tens and ones / 67

3.3　Ordering numbers up to 20 / 69

3.4　Addition and subtraction (I) / 71

3.5　Addition and subtraction (II) (1)
/ 73

3.6　Addition and subtraction (II) (2)
/ 75

3.7　Addition and subtraction (II) (3)
/ 77

3.8　Addition and subtraction (II) (4)
/ 79

3.9　Addition and subtraction (II) (5)
/ 81

Contents

3.10 Let's talk and calculate (III) / 83
3.11 Adding on and taking away / 85
3.12 Number walls / 87
Unit test 3 / 89

Chapter 4   Recognising shapes

4.1 Shapes of objects (1) / 91
4.2 Shapes of objects (2) / 93
Unit test 4 / 95

Chapter 5   Consolidation and enhancement

5.1 Sorting shapes / 98
5.2 Calculation with reasoning / 100
5.3 Comparing numbers / 102
5.4 Half and quarter / 104
5.5 Let's do addition together / 106
5.6 Let's do subtraction together / 108
5.7 Making number sentences / 110
5.8 Mathematics playground (1) / 112
5.9 Mathematics playground (2) / 114
5.10 Mathematics playground (3) / 116
Unit test 5 / 118

Chapter 6   Numbers up to 100

6.1 Tens and ones / 122
6.2 Knowing 100 / 124
6.3 Representing numbers up to 100 (1) / 126
6.4 Representing numbers up to 100 (2) / 128

6.5 Comparing numbers within 100 (1) / 130
6.6 Comparing numbers within 100 (2) / 132
6.7 Practice and exercise (I) / 134
6.8 Knowing money (1) / 136
6.9 Knowing money (2) / 138
Unit test 6 / 140

Chapter 7   Introduction to time（Ⅰ）

7.1 Year, month and day / 143
7.2 Telling the time / 145
7.3 Hour and half an hour / 147
Unit test 7 / 149

Chapter 8   Let's practise geometry

8.1 Left and right (1) / 152
8.2 Left and right (2) / 154
8.3 Left, centre and right, top, middle and bottom / 156
8.4 Comparing lengths / 158
8.5 Length and height (1) / 160
8.6 Length and height (2) / 162
8.7 Practice and exercise (II) / 164
Unit test 8 / 167

End of year test / 169

Answers / 175

Chapter 1 Numbers up to 10

1.1 Let's begin

 Learning objective

Count and match objects to 10

 Basic questions

1 Draw a line to match each pair.

2 Count and then match.

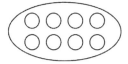   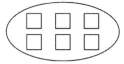   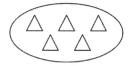   

③ Look at the picture, count and then fill in the blanks.

Challenge and extension question

④ How will you continue to colour the last three faces?

1.2   Let's sort (1)

Learning objective

Sort objects by 2 or more criteria

Basic questions

1 Sort the objects into two sets. Put a " √ " for toys and a " △ " for stationery.

( )   ( )   ( )   ( )

( )   ( )   ( )   ( )

( )   ( )   ( )   ( )

2 Let the animals and plants go back to the places they live. (Draw a line to link them.)

❸ Circle the one that does not belong to the group.

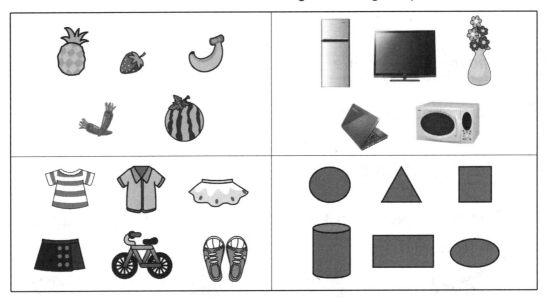

 Challenge and extension question

❹ Sort the toys. Write the numbers in the boxes.

| 1 | 2 | 3 | 4 | 5 |

| 6 | 7 | 8 | 9 | 10 |

You may sort them in the following way:

In the air:		

You can also sort them in another way:

1.3 Let's sort (2)

Sort objects in different ways

 Basic questions

1 Sort and circle.

(a)

(b)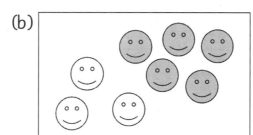

(c)

(d)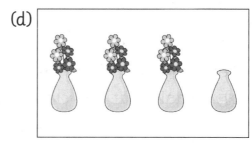

(e)

(f)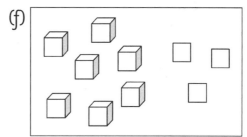

(g)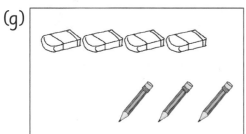

(h)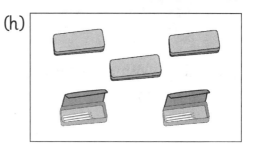

2 Sort the objects in different ways.

(a)

(b)

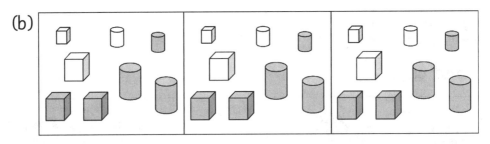

 Challenge and extension question

3 Link the animals to the circles.

(a) Animals with four legs are in Circle A.

(b) Animals that can climb trees are in Circle B.

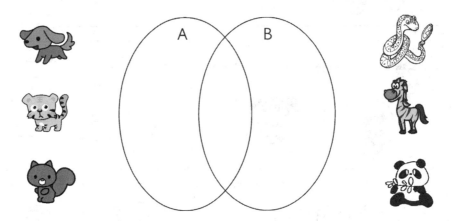

(c) Think: Which animal(s) should be in both Circle A and Circle B?

1.4 Let's count (1)

 Learning objective

Count and recognise numerals to 10

 Basic question

1 Count and match. The first one has been done for you.

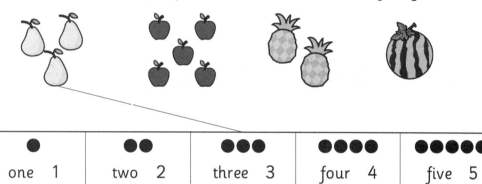

| one 1 | two 2 | three 3 | four 4 | five 5 |

| six 6 | seven 7 | eight 8 | nine 9 | ten 10 |

Challenge and extension question

2 Count and colour. The first one has been done for you.

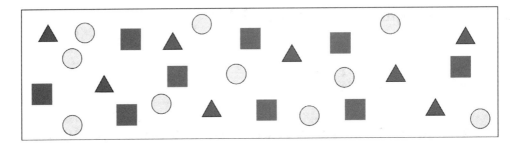

1.5 Let's count (2)

 Learning objective

Count and write numbers to 10

 Basic questions

1 Count and match. Then colour the dots and write the number in the space below (two and eight have been written for you as examples).

1 one	2 two	3 three	4 four	5 five

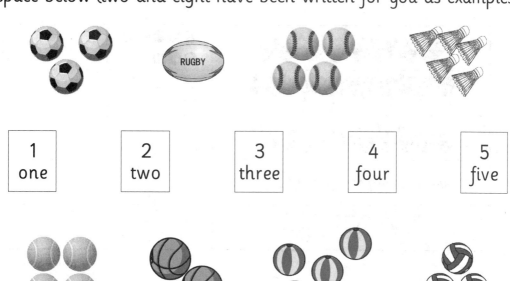

🏀🏀	●●○○○	two	2
⚽⚽⚽	○○○○○		
RUGBY	○○○○○		
🏸🏸🏸🏸🏸	○○○○○		
🎾🎾🎾🎾	○○○○○		

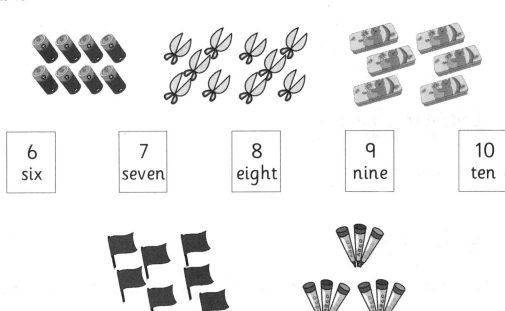

		eight	8

Challenge and extension question

2 Count the shapes and write the number in the (   ).

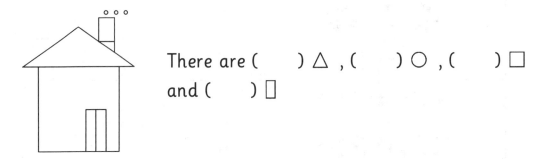

There are (   ) △ , (   ) ○ , (   ) □

and (   ) ⬠

1.6   Let's count (3)

Learning objective

Sort and count shapes

Basic questions

1 Sort the objects. Put the numbers of the objects into the oval shapes on the right.

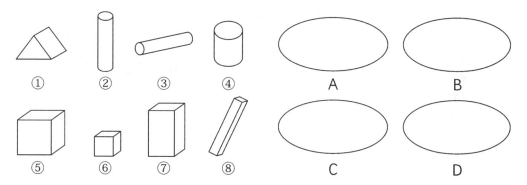

2 Count the colours and shapes and then write the results in the table.

(a)

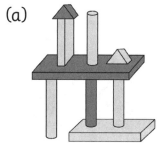

~~blue~~	( )	△	( )
~~grey~~	( )	⬡	( )
		▱	( )

(b)

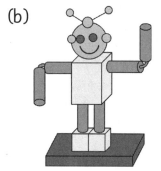

~~blue~~	( )	▢	( )
~~grey~~	( )	▭	( )
~~white~~	( )	▱	( )
~~dark~~	( )	●	( )

(c)

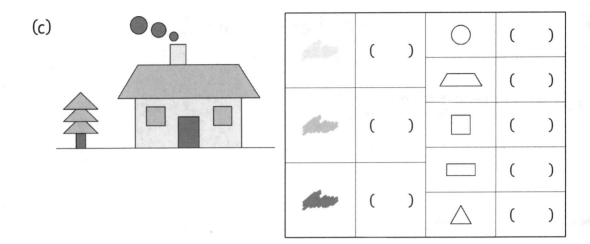

Challenge and extension question

❸ Find each diagram made up of 5 small cubes and put a "√" in the brackets.

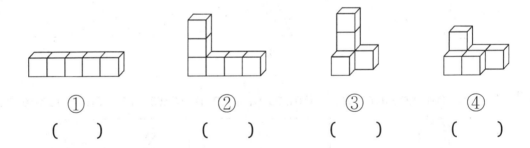

①　　　　　　②　　　　　　③　　　　　　④
(　)　　　　(　)　　　　(　)　　　　(　)

1.7   Let's count (4)

 Learning objective

Count groups of up to 10 objects

 Basic questions

1 Count the objects and write the numbers in the boxes.

☐

☐

☐

☐

☐

☐

2 Read the numbers and colour the dots. The first one has been done for you.

3 How much is two fives?

☐   ☐   ☐

4 Count and circle 10 items in each group.

 Challenge and extension question

5 Find and count the number of cubes in the diagram.

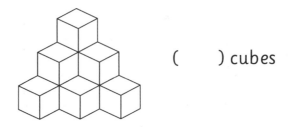

(   ) cubes

1.8   Let's count (5)

Learning objective

Count and recognise numbers to 10, including zero

Basic questions

1 Look at the pictures and write the numbers in the boxes.

(a) How many pears are on each tree?

(b) How many apples are in each plate?

2 Count the dots and write the numbers in the brackets.

⚪ ⚪ ⚪⚪⚪ ⚪				
( )	( )	( )	( )	( )

3 Draw the correct number of △ in the spaces below. The first one has been done for you.

△ △				
2	10	0	7	4

 Challenge and extension question

4 Look at your ruler and find the place where "0" is. Can you think what it stands for?

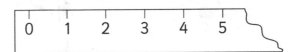

5 Fill in each box with a suitable number.

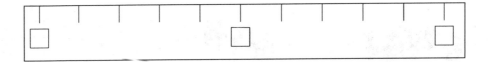

1.9 Let's count (6)

Learning objective

Count and partition numbers to 10

Basic questions

① Count and then fill in the blanks.

8

● ○ ●
● ○ ●
●

●__ ○__

6

○ ● ○
○
● ●

●__ ○__

9

● ○ ○
● ○ ●
● ○

●__ ○__

5

○ ○
●
○ ○

●__ ○__

10

● ●
○ ● ○ ●
● ○ ○

●__ ○__

7

● ○
● ●
○ ● ●

●__ ○__

② Colour the dots and write down the numbers. The second one has been done for you.

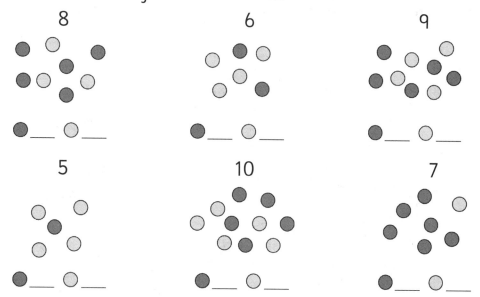

♥ ○		♥	○
♡ ♡ ♡ ♡ ♡	○○○○○		
♥ ♡ ♡ ♡ ♡	●○○○○	1	4
♥ ♥ ♡ ♡ ♡	○○○○○		
♥ ♥ ♥ ♡ ♡	○○○○○		
♥ ♥ ♥ ♥ ♡	○○○○○		
♥ ♥ ♥ ♥ ♥	○○○○○		

❸ Draw the correct number of dots to the other side of each oval.

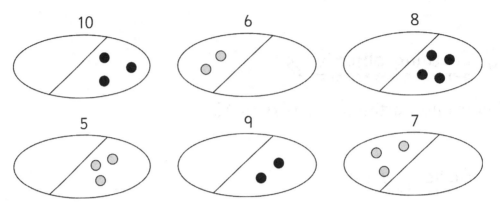

❹ Draw and then fill in the boxes.

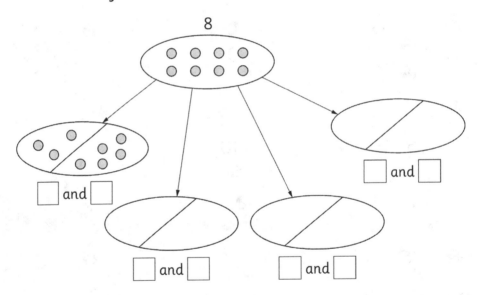

![Challenge and extension question]

Challenge and extension question

❺ Look for patterns and fill in with suitable numbers.

2		4		6		8			
1	1	2	2	3	3				

1.10 Counting and ordering numbers (1)

 Learning objective

Count and order numbers to 10

 Basic questions

1 Look at the pictures and fill in the brackets.

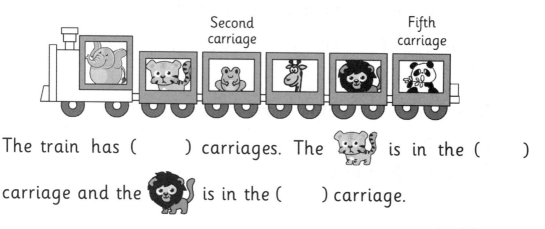

Second carriage

Fifth carriage

The train has (   ) carriages. The 🐯 is in the (   ) carriage and the 🦁 is in the (   ) carriage.

2 Count and then fill in the brackets.

(a)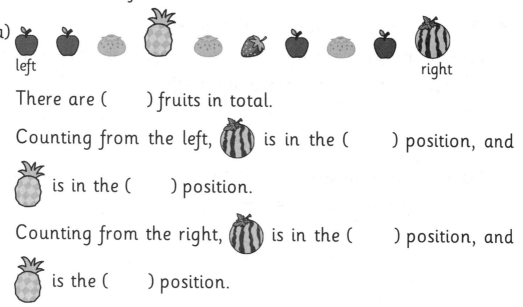

left   right

There are (   ) fruits in total.

Counting from the left, 🍉 is in the (   ) position, and 🍍 is in the (   ) position.

Counting from the right, 🍉 is in the (   ) position, and 🍍 is the (   ) position.

(b)

Counting from the left, is in the (   ) position.

Counting from the right, is in the (   ) position.

There are (   ) animals in total.

is in the middle. There are (   ) animals on its left.

There are (   ) animals on its right.

There are (   ) animals on the left of .

3 Count and colour. Start from the left.

Colour five of the hearts ♡ ♡ ♡ ♡ ♡ ♡

Colour the fifth heart ♡ ♡ ♡ ♡ ♡ ♡

Challenge and extension question

4 Draw the missing shapes in the boxes.

(a) Starting from the left to the right, ▲ is in the fourth place.
How many △ are there on its left?

▲ △ △ △ △

(b) Starting from the right to the left, ● is in the third place.
How many ○ are there on its right?

○ ○ ○ ●

1.11　Counting and ordering numbers (2)

 Learning objective

Write ordinal numbers to 10

 Basic questions

1 Count the birds.

There are (　　) 🐦 in total.

Counting from the left, colour the fourth 🐦 yellow and all

the 🐦 after the sixth one yellow. There are (　　) coloured

🐦 in total.

2 Put heights in order starting from the tallest. One has been done for you.

(　　) (　　　) (first) (　　) (　　)

3 Look at the picture and then fill in the brackets.

Number 1	Number 2	Number 3	Number 4	Number 5	Number 6
( ) place	( ) place	( ) place	( ) place	( ) place	( ) place

4 Draw figures according to the instruction.

Counting from the left, draw one $\triangle$ in the 5th place, one $\bigcirc$ in the 10th place, one $\square$ in the 3rd place, and finally two $\heartsuit$ in the 7th place.

Challenge and extension question

5 Put the pictures into the correct order. One has been done for you.

(   )   (first)   (   )   (   )

1.12   Let's compare (1)

📖 **Learning objective**

Compare sets to find more or fewer

✏️ **Basic questions**

① Compare the two sets. Put a tick (√) for the set that has more.

(a)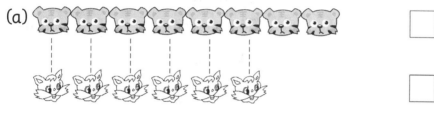

☐

☐

(b)

☐

☐

② Compare the three sets. Put a tick (√) for the set that has the most.

(a)

☐

☐

☐

(b)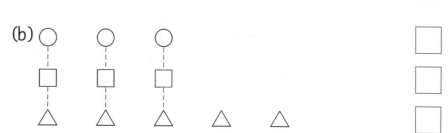

☐

☐

☐

3 Compare and then fill in the blanks.

There is _____ fewer than ▱.

There is _____ more ▱ than .

There are _____ ☆.

There are _____ ★.

There are _____ fewer ☆ than ★.

There are _____ more ★ than ☆.

4 Compare and then draw.
On the first line, draw 4 ○.
On the second line, draw △,
so it has 3 more than ○.
On the third line, draw □,
so it has 2 fewer than ○.

_____

_____

_____

Challenge and extension question

5 Think first and then colour the longest pencil.

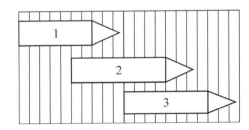

1.13 Let's compare (2)

Compare sets using greater than or less than

 Basic questions

1 Look at the pictures. Fill in the ◯ with ">" (greater than), "<" (less than) or "=" (equal to).

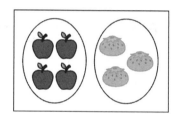 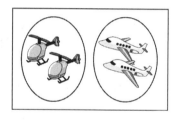 

4 ◯ 3   2 ◯ 2   1 ◯ 5

2 Look at the pictures and fill in with your answers.

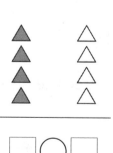

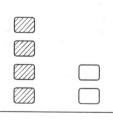

☐ ◯ ☐   ☐ ◯ ☐   ☐ ◯ ☐

3 Compare, draw and then fill in the boxes below.

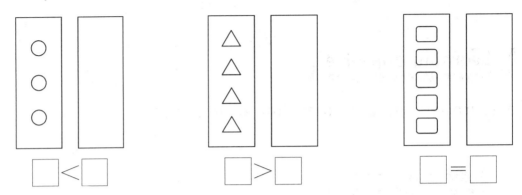

□ < □   □ > □   □ = □

4 Fill in the ◯ with ">", "<" or "=".

4 ◯ 6   8 ◯ 5   7 ◯ 4   9 ◯ 9

8 ◯ 2   7 ◯ 8   6 ◯ 6   0 ◯ 10

5 Fill in the boxes with suitable numbers.

5 < □   8 > □   7 = □   9 > □

□ > 7   □ < 10   □ < 6   □ = 8

9 > □ > □   2 < □ < □

 Challenge and extension question

6 Which glass of water tastes the sweetest after the cube of sugar is put in? Put a "√" in the bracket.

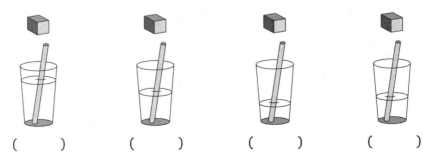

(   )   (   )   (   )   (   )

1.14   The number line

 Learning objective

Identify numbers to 10 on a number line

Basic questions

1 Which of the following show a complete number line (without an ending point)? Put a "√" in the (   ) to indicate your answer.

(a) 0 1 2 3 4 5 6 7 8 9 10   (   )

(b) 0 1 2 3 4 5 6 7 8 →   (   )

(c) 1 2 3 4 5 6 7 8 9 10 11   (   )

(d) 0 2 4 6 8 10 →   (   )

2 Fill in the boxes with correct numbers.

(a) 0 1 ☐ ☐ ☐ ☐ ☐ ☐ 8 ☐ 10

(b) ☐ 2 ☐ ☐ 8 ☐

3 Fill in the blanks. (Note: one unit on a number line is the distance between any two neighbouring numbers, for example, from 0 to 1.)

(a)

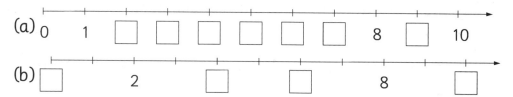

jumps _____ times. It jumps _____ units

each time. It jumps _____ units altogether.

(b)

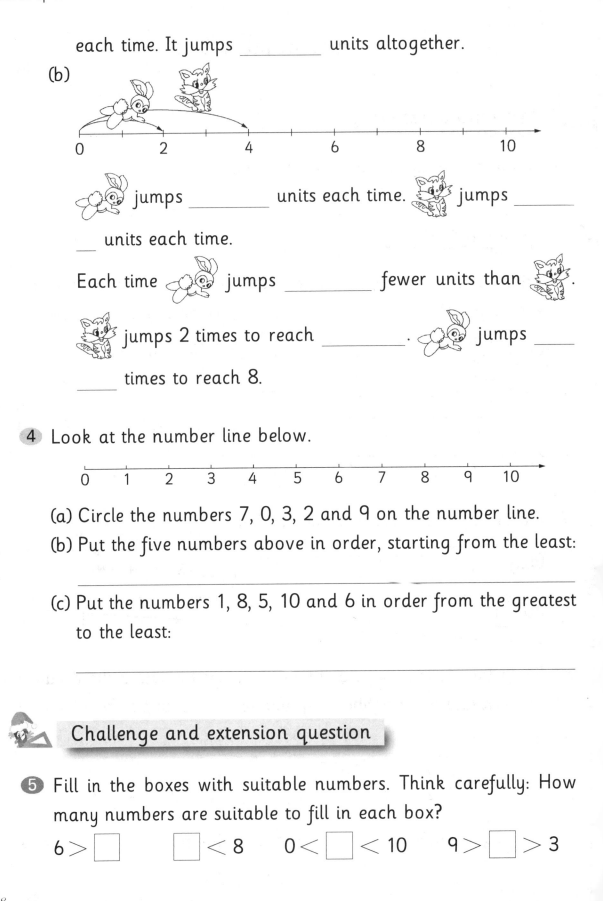

🐰 jumps _____ units each time. 🐱 jumps _____ ___ units each time.

Each time 🐰 jumps _____ fewer units than 🐱.

🐱 jumps 2 times to reach _____. 🐰 jumps ____ _____ times to reach 8.

4 Look at the number line below.

0 1 2 3 4 5 6 7 8 9 10

(a) Circle the numbers 7, 0, 3, 2 and 9 on the number line.

(b) Put the five numbers above in order, starting from the least:

_____

(c) Put the numbers 1, 8, 5, 10 and 6 in order from the greatest to the least:

_____

Challenge and extension question

5 Fill in the boxes with suitable numbers. Think carefully: How many numbers are suitable to fill in each box?

6 > ☐   ☐ < 8   0 < ☐ < 10   9 > ☐ > 3

Unit test 1

1 Match the pairs. The first one has been done for you.

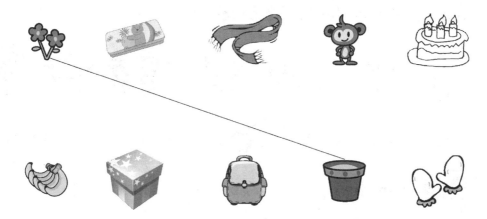

2 Count and draw lines to match.

3 Sort the objects into two sets using different ways.

4 Count and then fill in the brackets.

Starting from the left, is in the (   ) place and

 is in the (   ) place.

Starting from the right, is in the (   ) place and

is in the (   ) place.
There are (   ) animals in total.

5 Count and then colour.
(a) Start from the left.

Colour four of the apples

Colour the fourth apple

(b) Start from the right.
Colour the fifth strawberry
Colour five of the strawberries

6 Put the cars in the correct order.

There are _____ cars in total.

In first place is car number _____ .

Car number 5 is in the _____ place.

Car number 1 is in the _____ place.

In third place is car number _____ .

7 Put the pictures in the correct order.

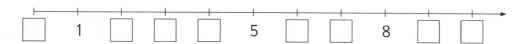

8 Fill in each box to complete the number line.

☐ 1 ☐ ☐ ☐ 5 ☐ ☐ 8 ☐ ☐

9 Write the numbers in the boxes and brackets below.

(a)

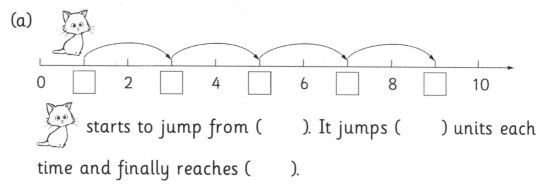

0 ☐ 2 ☐ 4 ☐ 6 ☐ 8 ☐ 10

starts to jump from (   ). It jumps (   ) units each

time and finally reaches (   ).

(b)

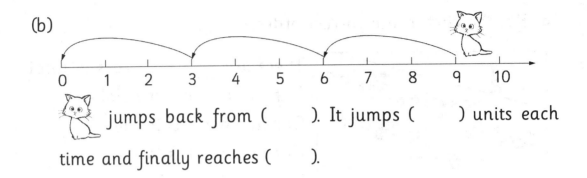

jumps back from (   ). It jumps (   ) units each time and finally reaches (   ).

10 Look at the pictures and compare.

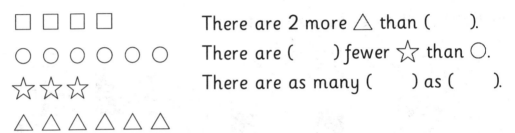

There are 2 more △ than (   ).

There are (   ) fewer ☆ than ○.

There are as many (   ) as (   ).

11 Fill in the ◯ with ">", "<" or "=" and the ☐ with suitable numbers.

5 ◯ 7   9 ◯ 6   4 ◯ 4   10 ◯ 5 ◯ 0

8 = ☐   ☐ < 8   7 > ☐   ☐ < 6 < ☐

☐ = ☐   ☐ < ☐   ☐ > ☐   8 ◯ ☐ ◯ 1

12 Put the numbers in order.

(a) From the least to the greatest: 5, 8, 10, 4, 9 and 2.

_____

(b) From the greatest to the least: 4, 7, 1, 6, 0 and 10.

_____

Chapter 2   Addition and subtraction within 10

2.1   Number bonds

 Learning objective

Represent number bonds to 10

 Basic questions

1 Fill in the following tables. The first row has been done for you.

○○○○	0	4
●○○○		
●●○○		
●●●○		
●●●●		

●○○○○		
●●○○○		
●●●○○		
●●●●○		
●●●●●		

2 Circle the objects and complete the number bonds.

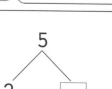

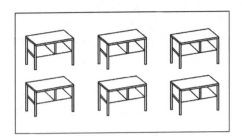

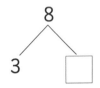

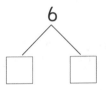

3 Fill in the boxes.

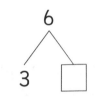

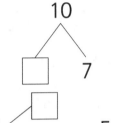

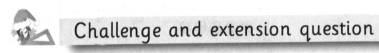

Challenge and extension question

4 Think carefully and then fill in the brackets with suitable numbers.

(a) $5 + 1 = (4) + (2) = ($ $) + ($ $) = ($ $) + ($ $)$

     $= ($ $) + ($ $)$

(b) $9 + 1 = (8) + (2) = ($ $) + ($ $) = ($ $) + ($ $)$

     $= ($ $) + ($ $) = ($ $) + ($ $) = ($ $) + ($ $)$

     $= ($ $) + ($ $) = ($ $) + ($ $) = ($ $) + ($ $)$

     $= ($ $) + ($ $)$

2.2 Addition (1)

 Learning objective

Add pairs of numbers with a total to 10

 Basic questions

1 Fill in the boxes.

5 ╲╱ 3   1 ╲╱ 8   2 ╲╱ 3   8 ╲╱ 2   4 ╲╱ 6

☐   ☐   ☐   ☐   ☐

2 Look at the pictures and then fill in the boxes. The first one has been done for you.

$3 + 4 = 7$

$4 + 3 = 7$

☐ + ☐ = ☐

☐ + ☐ = ☐

☐ + ☐ = ☐

☐ + ☐ = ☐

☐ + ☐ = ☐

☐ + ☐ = ☐

☐ + ☐ = ☐
☐ + ☐ = ☐

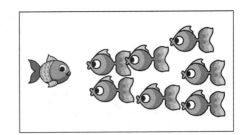

☐ + ☐ = ☐
☐ + ☐ = ☐

❸ Fill in the following tables.

Addend	8	2	5	1	3
Addend	2	4	3	9	3
Sum					

Addend	7	5	4	2	6
Addend	1	5	3	1	4
Sum					

4 Draw a line to link the additions with the same sum.

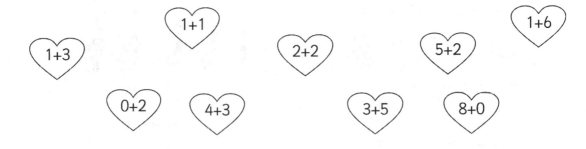

1+1
1+3
2+2
5+2
1+6
0+2
4+3
3+5
8+0

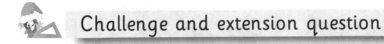

Challenge and extension question

❺ Write addition calculations with a total of 5.

☐ + ☐ = 5   ☐ + ☐ = 5

☐ + ☐ = 5   ☐ + ☐ = 5

☐ + ☐ = 5   ☐ + ☐ = 5

2.3 Addition (2)

Add pairs of numbers with a total to 10

 Basic questions

1 Let's think.

(a) Write each sum.

○ ○ ○ ○
○ ○ ○ ○
0 + 8 = ____

● ○ ○ ○
○ ○ ○ ○
1 + ____ = ____

● ● ○ ○
○ ○ ○ ○
____ + ____ = ____

● ● ● ○
○ ○ ○ ○
____ + ____ = ____

● ● ● ●
○ ○ ○ ○
____ + ____ = ____

● ● ● ●
● ○ ○ ○
____ + ____ = ____

● ● ● ●
● ● ○ ○
____ + ____ = ____

● ● ● ●
● ● ● ○
____ + ____ = ____

● ● ● ●
● ● ● ●
____ + ____ = ____

(b) Colour the dots to show different sums of 9.

● ● ● ● ●
● ● ● ●
9 + 0 = 9

○ ○ ○ ○ ○
○ ○ ○ ○
1 + ____ = ____

○ ○ ○ ○ ○
○ ○ ○ ○
____ + ____ = ____

○ ○ ○ ○ ○
○ ○ ○ ○
____ + ____ = ____

○ ○ ○ ○ ○
○ ○ ○ ○
____ + ____ = ____

○ ○ ○ ○ ○
○ ○ ○ ○
____ + ____ = ____

○ ○ ○ ○ ○
○ ○ ○ ○
____ + ____ = ____

○ ○ ○ ○ ○
○ ○ ○ ○
____ + ____ = ____

○ ○ ○ ○ ○
○ ○ ○ ○
____ + ____ = ____

2 Fill in the blanks.

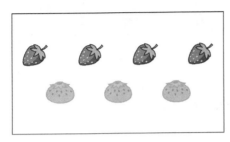

$4 + 3 = $ _____

_____ $+$ _____ $=$ _____

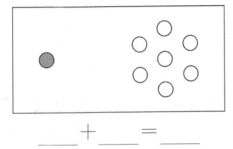

_____ $+$ _____ $=$ _____

_____ $+$ _____ $=$ _____

3 Work out the sums.

$3 + 5 =$	$4 + 6 =$	$2 + 5 =$	$0 + 4 =$
$4 + 4 =$	$5 + 1 =$	$2 + 2 =$	$6 + 2 =$
$2 + 8 =$	$3 + 3 =$	$6 + 3 =$	$5 + 4 =$

 Challenge and extension question

4 Look at the picture. How many addition sentences can you write?

_____

_____

_____

_____

_____

2.4 Addition (3)

Add to 10 by combining

 Basic questions

1 Look at the pictures and write the addition sentences.

There were   Another 4 rabbits   How many rabbits
6 rabbits.   join them.   are there now?

   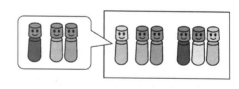

2 Fill in the brackets. The first one has been done for you.

(a) $2 \xrightarrow{+5} (7)$ $1 \xrightarrow{+2} (\quad)$ $4 \xrightarrow{+4} (\quad)$

$5 \xrightarrow{+1} (\quad)$ $6 \xrightarrow{+3} (\quad)$ $7 \xrightarrow{+0} (\quad)$

$(\quad) \xrightarrow{+5} 10$ $(\quad) \xrightarrow{+7} 8$ $(\quad) \xrightarrow{+6} 9$

$7 \xrightarrow{(\quad)} 10$ $2 \xrightarrow{(\quad)} 8$ $5 \xrightarrow{(\quad)} 5$

(b)

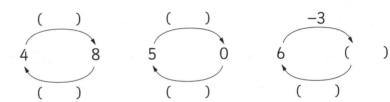

3 Work out the sums.

$6+2=$	$3+5=$	$4+4=$	$5+0=$
$7+1=$	$5+4=$	$2+6=$	$3+2=$
$0+10=$	$7+3=$	$3+3=$	$0+4=$
$1+9=$	$6+3=$	$0+8=$	$2+4=$

Challenge and extension question

4 Think carefully and then fill in the brackets.

(a) If $\star + \maltese = 8$ and $5 + \maltese = 7$, then $\star = (\quad)$. $\maltese = (\quad)$.

(b) If $\bigcirc = \star\star\star$ and $\star = \triangle\triangle$, then $\bigcirc = (\quad)\triangle$.

2.5 Let's talk and calculate (I)

 Learning objective

Write addition sentences with totals to 10

Basic questions

① Look at the pictures and write the addition sentences.

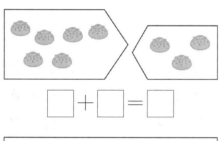

□+□=□

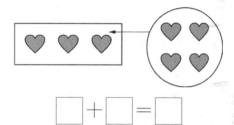

□+□=□

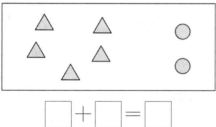

□+□=□

How many are altogether?

□+□=□

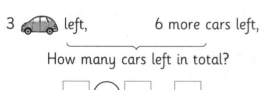 3 🚗 left,   6 more cars left,

How many cars left in total?

□◯□=□

4 🍎 were eaten,   2 are left,

How many were there at first?

□◯□=□

Sort by colour:

(   )+(   )=(   )

(   )+(   )=(   )

Sort by size:

(   )+(   )=(   )

(   )+(   )=(   )

2 Fill in the boxes.

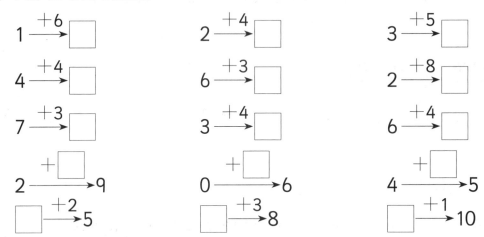

$1 \xrightarrow{+6} \square$ $2 \xrightarrow{+4} \square$ $3 \xrightarrow{+5} \square$

$4 \xrightarrow{+4} \square$ $6 \xrightarrow{+3} \square$ $2 \xrightarrow{+8} \square$

$7 \xrightarrow{+3} \square$ $3 \xrightarrow{+4} \square$ $6 \xrightarrow{+4} \square$

$2 \xrightarrow{+\square} 9$ $0 \xrightarrow{+\square} 6$ $4 \xrightarrow{+\square} 5$

$\square \xrightarrow{+2} 5$ $\square \xrightarrow{+3} 8$ $\square \xrightarrow{+1} 10$

3 Work out the sums.

$2+3=$ $5+4=$ $1+4=$ $6+2=$

$4+0=$ $3+7=$ $4+2=$ $5+4=$

$3+3=$ $5+2=$ $3+6=$ $0+7=$

$6+4=$ $3+4=$ $4+5=$ $8+2=$

 Challenge and extension question

4 Look at the picture and write the addition sentences.

How many can you write?

2.6   Subtraction (1)

Learning objective

Subtract within 10 by taking away

Basic questions

1 Look at the pictures and write the subtraction sentences.

  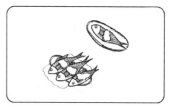

There were 6 fish   The cat ate 2 fish.   How many fish are
in the plate.   left now?

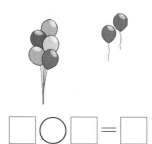

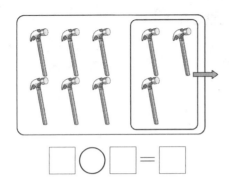

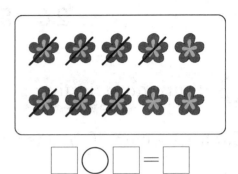

☐ ◯ ☐ = ☐   ☐ ◯ ☐ = ☐

2 Calculate.

$8 - 4 =$ $10 - 9 =$ $6 - 4 =$ $2 - 2 =$

$4 - 3 =$ $5 - 2 =$ $9 - 4 =$ $6 - 1 =$

$10 - 5 =$ $8 - 7 =$ $7 - 5 =$ $8 - 6 =$

$5 - 5 =$ $2 - 0 =$ $4 - 1 =$ $9 - 6 =$

3 Fill in the tables. (Note: minuend − subtrahend = difference)

Minuend	8	10	5	9	3
Subtrahend	2	4	3	1	3
Difference					

Minuend	7	5	4	2	6
Subtrahend	1	5	3	1	4
Difference					

Challenge and extension question

4 Write subtraction calculations with a difference of 5.

☐ − ☐ = 5   ☐ − ☐ = 5

☐ − ☐ = 5   ☐ − ☐ = 5

☐ − ☐ = 5   ☐ − ☐ = 5

2.7   Subtraction (2)

 Learning objective

Subtract within 10 using known addition bonds

 Basic questions

1 Fill in the boxes. The first one has been done for you.

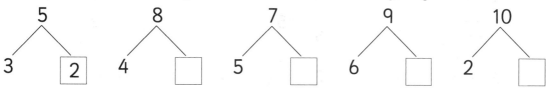

5
3   [2]

8
4   [ ]

7
5   [ ]

9
6   [ ]

10
2   [ ]

2 Look at the pictures and fill in the boxes.

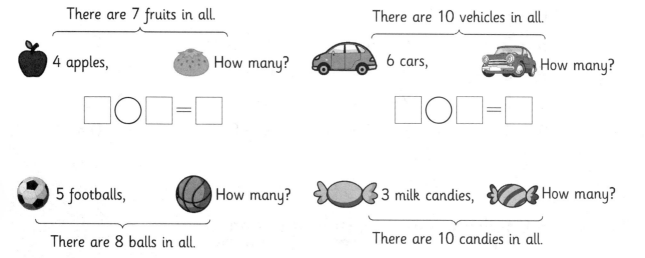

There are 7 fruits in all.

4 apples,   How many?

☐ ◯ ☐ = ☐

There are 10 vehicles in all.

6 cars,   How many?

☐ ◯ ☐ = ☐

5 footballs,   How many?

There are 8 balls in all.

☐ ◯ ☐ = ☐

3 milk candies,   How many?

There are 10 candies in all.

☐ ◯ ☐ = ☐

How many apples are inside?

Fruit

There are 9 apples in all.

$\square \bigcirc \square = \square$

How many books are inside?

There are 7 books in all.

$\square \bigcirc \square = \square$

③ Fill in the brackets.

$5 \xrightarrow{-2} (\quad)$ $\qquad$ $4 \xrightarrow{-3} (\quad)$ $\qquad$ $8 \xrightarrow{-6} (\quad)$

$9 \xrightarrow{-1} (\quad)$ $\qquad$ $6 \xrightarrow{-5} (\quad)$ $\qquad$ $10 \xrightarrow{-2} (\quad)$

$6 \xrightarrow{-3} (\quad)$ $\qquad$ $7 \xrightarrow{-7} (\quad)$ $\qquad$ $9 \xrightarrow{-4} (\quad)$

$10 \xrightarrow{(\quad)} 6$ $\qquad$ $8 \xrightarrow{(\quad)} 5$ $\qquad$ $7 \xrightarrow{(\quad)} 1$

④ Calculate.

$6-2=$ $\qquad$ $4-4=$ $\qquad$ $5-0=$ $\qquad$ $7-2=$

$7-6=$ $\qquad$ $9-4=$ $\qquad$ $6-3=$ $\qquad$ $3-2=$

$5-2=$ $\qquad$ $7-3=$ $\qquad$ $9-6=$ $\qquad$ $10-5=$

$9-1=$ $\qquad$ $6-5=$ $\qquad$ $8-8=$ $\qquad$ $2-0=$

 Challenge and extension question

⑤ Think carefully and then fill in the brackets. (Note: look for a pattern to help you.)

$2-0=(3)-(1)=(\quad)-(\quad)=(\quad)-(\quad)=(\quad)-(\quad)$

$=(\quad)-(\quad)=(\quad)-(\quad)=(\quad)-(\quad)=(\quad)-(\quad)$

2.8　Subtraction (3)

Subtract within 10 using known addition bonds

 Basic questions

1 Look at the pictures and write the subtraction sentences.

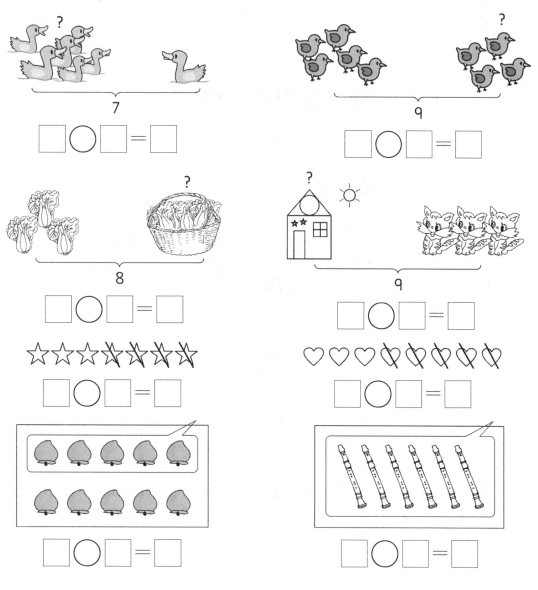

2 Fill in the boxes.

$8 \xrightarrow{-4} \square$ $10 \xrightarrow{-5} \square$ $6 \xrightarrow{-3} \square$

$5 \xrightarrow{-2} \square$ $7 \xrightarrow{-3} \square$ $8 \xrightarrow{-2} \square$

$\square \xrightarrow{-2} 5$ $\square \xrightarrow{-3} 0$ $\square \xrightarrow{-1} 9$

3 Calculate.

$8 - 5 =$ $10 - 4 =$ $4 - 4 =$ $6 - 0 =$

$6 - 3 =$ $8 - 7 =$ $9 - 6 =$ $8 - 3 =$

$8 - 1 =$ $5 - 2 =$ $7 - 6 =$ $10 - 7 =$

 Challenge and extension question

4 Look at the picture and then write the number sentences.

How many fish did the white cat and black cat catch altogether?

$\square \bigcirc \square = \square$

How many more fish did the white cat catch than the black cat?

$\square \bigcirc \square = \square$

How many more fish does the black cat need to catch in order to have as many fish as the white cat has caught?

$\square \bigcirc \square = \square$

2.9 Let's talk and calculate (II)

Interpret word problems using subtraction facts to 10

 Basic questions

① Look at the pictures and complete the number sentences.

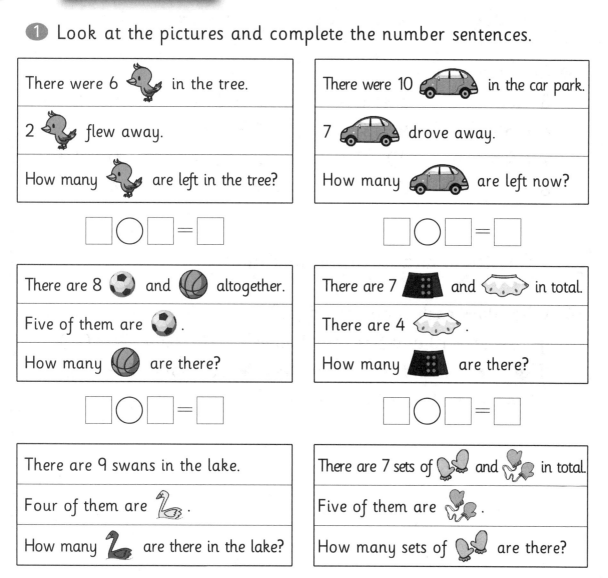

2 Fill in the boxes.

$10 \xrightarrow{-6} \square$ $8 \xrightarrow{-4} \square$ $7 \xrightarrow{-5} \square$ $7 \xrightarrow{-4} \square$

$6 \xrightarrow{-3} \square$ $9 \xrightarrow{-8} \square$ $\square \xrightarrow{-1} 6$ $5 \xrightarrow{-\square} 4$

$8 \xrightarrow{-\square} 4$ $7 \xrightarrow{-\square} 5$ $\square \xrightarrow{-2} 7$ $4 \xrightarrow{-\square} 0$

$\square \xrightarrow{-2} 6$ $4 \xrightarrow{-\square} 3$ $9 \xrightarrow{-\square} 9$

3 Calculate.

$3-0=$ $5+4=$ $8-8=$ $9-5=$

$4+6=$ $9-3=$ $5+2=$ $10-3=$

$7+2=$ $10-7=$ $3-2=$ $0+1=$

$8-5=$ $5+5=$ $4-0=$ $4-2=$

 Challenge and extension question

4 What does each shape stand for?

If $\triangle + \star = 10$ and $8 - \star = 2$, then $\triangle = ($ $)$ and $\star = ($ $)$.

If $\blacklozenge - \blacksquare = 7$ and $\blacksquare + 3 = 5$, then $\blacklozenge = ($ $)$ and $\blacksquare = ($ $)$.

2.10 Addition and subtraction

Learning objective

Use the inverse relationship between addition and subtraction with numbers to 10

Basic questions

1 Look at the pictures and write the number sentences.

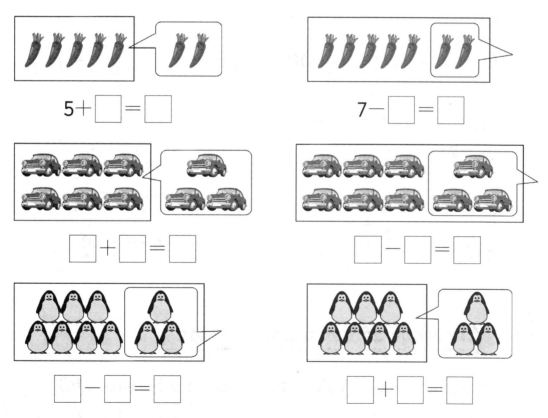

$5+\boxed{}=\boxed{}$

$7-\boxed{}=\boxed{}$

$\boxed{}+\boxed{}=\boxed{}$

$\boxed{}-\boxed{}=\boxed{}$

$\boxed{}-\boxed{}=\boxed{}$

$\boxed{}+\boxed{}=\boxed{}$

2 Fill in the boxes with suitable numbers.

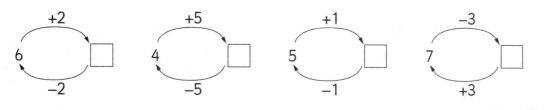

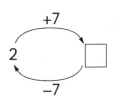   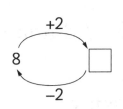   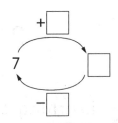

3 Fill in the boxes.

$4 + 1 = \square$ $2 + 3 = \square$ $4 + 6 = \square$

$5 - 4 = \square$ $5 - 2 = \square$ $10 - 4 = \square$

$5 - 1 = \square$ $5 - 3 = \square$ $10 - 6 = \square$

$8 + 1 = \square$ $3 + 7 = \square$ $5 + 2 = \square$

$9 - \square = \square$ $10 - \square = \square$ $\square - \square = \square$

$9 - \square = \square$ $10 - \square = \square$ $\square - \square = \square$

4 Calculate and fill in the boxes.

$3 \xrightarrow{+2} \square \xrightarrow{+4} \square$ $9 \xrightarrow{-2} \square \xrightarrow{-5} \square$

$4 \xrightarrow{+6} \square \xrightarrow{-5} \square$ $10 \xrightarrow{-7} \square \xrightarrow{+3} \square$

$5 \xrightarrow{+5} \square \xrightarrow{-6} \square$ $4 \xrightarrow{-4} \square \xrightarrow{+10} \square$

   Challenge and extension question

5 Write subtraction calculations with a difference of 3.

$\square - \square = 3$ $\square - \square = 3$

$\square - \square = 3$ $\square - \square = 3$

$\square - \square = 3$ $\square - \square = 3$

$\square - \square = 3$ $\square - \square = 3$

2.11 Addition and subtraction using a number line

Learning objective

Add and subtract numbers to 10 using a number line

Basic questions

1 Fill in the boxes to complete the number lines.

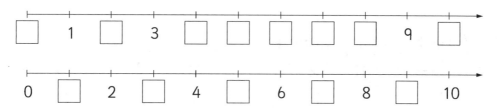

2 Calculate using a number line.

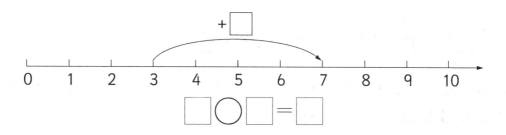

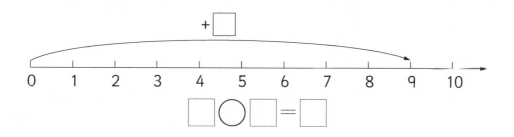

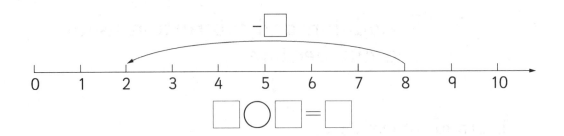

$$\square \bigcirc \square = \square$$

❸ Calculate.

$4+4=$	$9-3=$	$10-4=$	$3+6=$
$10-6=$	$5+5=$	$9+1=$	$9-7=$
$3+6=$	$3+7=$	$4+6=$	$3+4=$
$10-5=$	$7-7=$	$10-8=$	$8-4=$

4 Write the missing numbers.

$(\quad)+4=8 \qquad 2+(\quad)=10 \qquad 7-(\quad)=3$

$3+(\quad)=6 \qquad (\quad)+8=8 \qquad (\quad)-6=3$

$5+(\quad)=9 \qquad (\quad)-3=6 \qquad 8-(\quad)=10-4$

 Challenge and extension question

❺ Look at each number sentence below, draw it on the number line and find the answer.

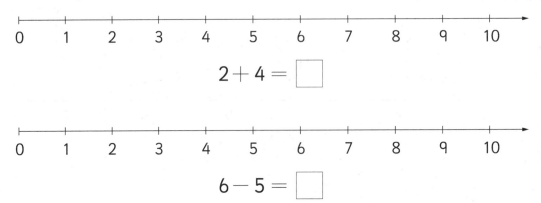

$$2+4=\square$$

$$6-5=\square$$

2.12 Games of number 10

Solve problems for pairs of numbers that total 10

 Basic questions

1 Which pairs of numbers make 10?

(2) — (9)   (5)   (10)

(1)   (7)   (8)   (5)

(3)   (6)   (0)   (4)

2 Fill in the ☐ with suitable numbers.

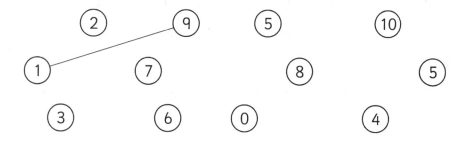

```
                    1 and ☐
                       |
 ☐ and 2 — (10) — ☐ and ☐
                       |
        3 and ☐      6 and ☐
```

3 Which key is for which lock? (Draw a line to link them.)

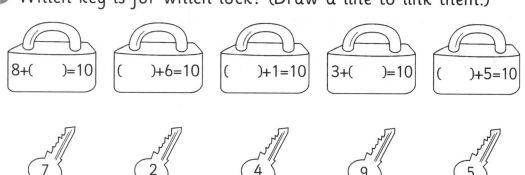

8+( )=10   ( )+6=10   ( )+1=10   3+( )=10   ( )+5=10

7   2   4   9   5

4 Draw a line to match.

2+8	2+7		7−5	7−4
4+5	5+3		9−3	6−4
2+6	3+4		8−4	9−5
9−2	3+7		6−3	8−2

5 Calculate.

$5+(\quad)=10$ $10-(\quad)=0$ $9+(\quad)=10$

$10-(\quad)=1$ $3+(\quad)=10$ $(\quad)+2=10$

$10=7+(\quad)$ $(\quad)-5=5$ $(\quad)+8=10$

$3+(\quad)=7$ $4+(\quad)=8$ $(\quad)-(\quad)=3$

6 Fill in the ◯ with ">", "<" or "=".

$7+3\bigcirc 8$ $5+4\bigcirc 7$ $2+7\bigcirc 5+3$

$4-2\bigcirc 6$ $9-3\bigcirc 6$ $5+3\bigcirc 9+0$

$2+8\bigcirc 10$ $8-5\bigcirc 10$ $6+4\bigcirc 5+5$

 Challenge and extension question

7 Write out addition sentences with totals of 10.

$10=\square+\square=\square+\square=\square+\square=\square+\square=\square+\square$

$=\square+\square+\square$

2.13 Adding three numbers

 Learning objective

Add three numbers with totals to 10

 Basic questions

1 Look at the pictures and write the number sentences.

?

□○□○□=□   □○□○□=□

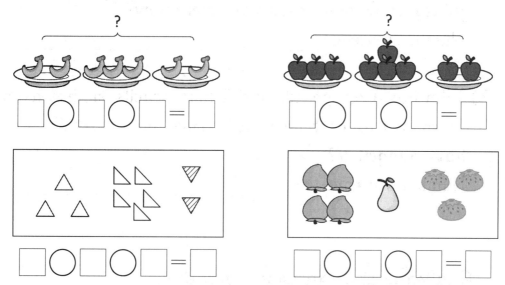

□○□○□=□   □○□○□=□

2 Look at the number lines and complete the calculations.

+□   +□

0   1   2   3   4   5   6   7   8   9   10

□○□○□=□

+□   +□

0   1   2   3   4   5   6   7   8   9   10

□○□○□=□

3 Work out the sums.

1 + 3 + 3 =	0 + 3 + 4 =	8 + 0 + 2 =
3 + 4 + 0 =	2 + 2 + 1 =	1 + 6 + 2 =
2 + 1 + 6 =	5 + 3 + 2 =	2 + 7 + 1 =
2 + 4 + 1 =	4 + 2 + 4 =	1 + 4 + 5 =

4 Write the number sentences.

(a) 3 chicks were playing in the grass field. Another 2 chicks from the left joined them. Then 5 more chicks from the right joined. How many chicks are there now?

Number sentence: _____

(b) John has 4 red pencils and 2 blue pencils. He has as many green pencils as blue pencils. How many pencils does he have altogether?

Number sentence: _____

 Challenge and extension question

5 Think carefully and then fill in the boxes.

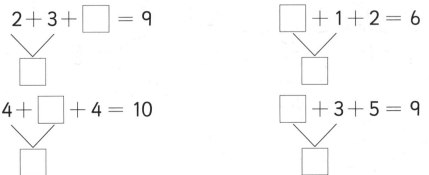

$2 + 3 + \boxed{} = 9$

$\boxed{} + 1 + 2 = 6$

$4 + \boxed{} + 4 = 10$

$\boxed{} + 3 + 5 = 9$

2.14 Subtracting three numbers

Subtract two smaller numbers from a number to 10

 Basic questions

① Look at the pictures and write the number sentences.

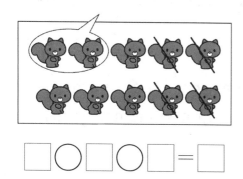

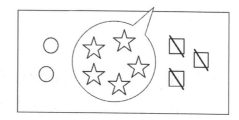

□○□○□=□   □○□○□=□

② Look at the number lines and complete the calculations.

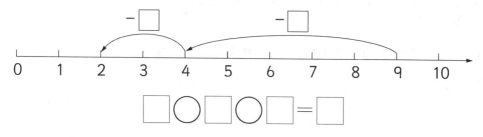

□○□○□=□

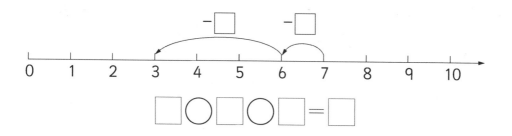

□○□○□=□

3 Calculate.

$5 - 3 - 1 =$	$6 - 3 - 3 =$	$8 - 4 - 2 =$
$6 - 4 - 0 =$	$7 - 2 - 1 =$	$9 - 3 - 5 =$
$8 - 7 - 1 =$	$10 - 3 - 4 =$	$10 - 7 - 3 =$
$8 - 2 - 2 =$	$7 - 2 - 3 =$	$6 - 3 - 1 =$
$10 - 6 - 2 =$	$6 - 5 - 1 =$	$4 - 2 - 2 =$

4 Read the problems and then write the number sentences.

(a) 9 birds were in the tree. 5 birds flew away. Then another 2 birds flew away. How many birds are still in the tree?

Number sentence: _____

(b) There are 9 balloons. 3 of them are blue. Another 4 are red. The rest are yellow. How many balloons are yellow?

Number sentence: _____

 Challenge and extension question

5 Think carefully and then fill in the boxes.

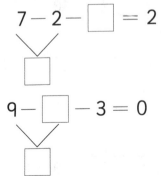

$7 - 2 - \square = 2$

$9 - \square - 3 = 0$

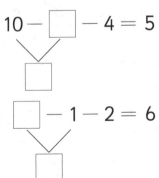

$10 - \square - 4 = 5$

$\square - 1 - 2 = 6$

2.15 Mixed addition and subtraction

 Learning objective

Add and subtract three numbers within 10

 Basic questions

1 Look at the pictures and write the number sentences.

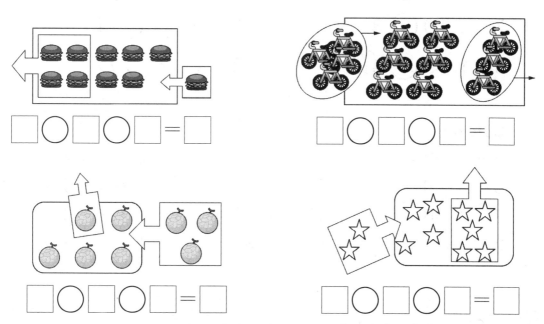

□ ◯ □ ◯ □ = □   □ ◯ □ ◯ □ = □

□ ◯ □ ◯ □ = □   □ ◯ □ ◯ □ = □

2 Look at the number lines and complete the calculations.

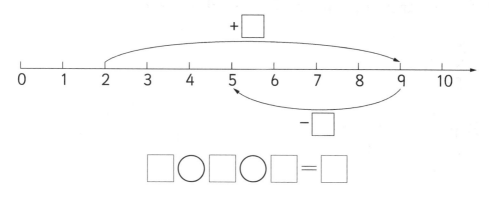

□ ◯ □ ◯ □ = □

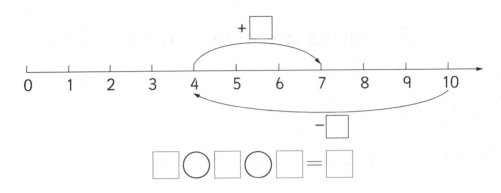

$$\boxed{}\bigcirc\boxed{}\bigcirc\boxed{}=\boxed{}$$

③ Fill in the $\bigcirc$ with ">", "<" or "=".

$5+2-3\bigcirc 8$ $\qquad$ $8-4+2\bigcirc 6$

$7-4+0\bigcirc 3$ $\qquad$ $10+0-7\bigcirc 2$

$6-1+5\bigcirc 4$ $\qquad$ $9-4+2\bigcirc 7$

④ Calculate.

$2+4+3=$ $\qquad$ $6-3+4=$ $\qquad$ $8-4+2=$

$6+4+0=$ $\qquad$ $2+2-1=$ $\qquad$ $1+6-5=$

$8-7-0=$ $\qquad$ $10-3+2=$ $\qquad$ $2+7-3=$

$2+5+1=$ $\qquad$ $4-2+8=$ $\qquad$ $6-4+5=$

Challenge and extension question

⑤ Think carefully and then fill in the boxes.

$4+4-\boxed{}=7$ $\qquad$ $\boxed{}-2+1=8$

$3+\boxed{}-2=6$ $\qquad$ $\boxed{}-1+2=2$

Unit test 2

1 Complete the mental sums.

$4+2=$	$9-4=$	$6-3=$	$5-5=$
$8-8=$	$3+6=$	$7-4=$	$6+4=$
$1+9=$	$9-7=$	$2+5=$	$10-5=$

2 Draw lines to link cat buddies.

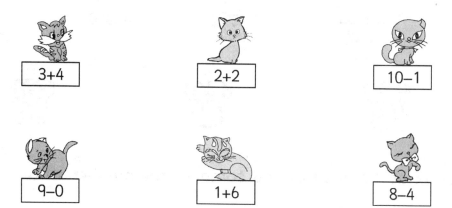

| 3+4 | 2+2 | 10−1 |

| 9−0 | 1+6 | 8−4 |

3 Look at the number lines and complete the calculations.

(a)

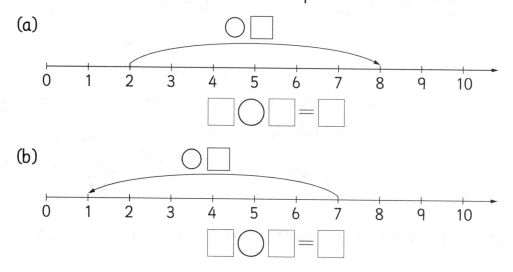

(b)

(c)

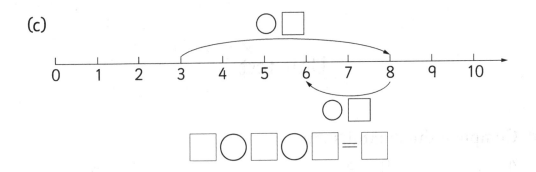

$$\square \bigcirc \square \square \bigcirc \square = \square$$

4 Draw a line to match each flower to a vase.

2+5+3   5+5−5   9−5+2   7−4+7

10−1−3   8−3+0   4+6−0   9−2−2

10   6   5

5 Look at the pictures and complete the number sentences.

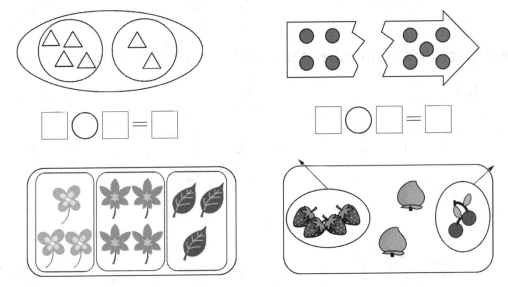

$$\square \bigcirc \square = \square \qquad \square \bigcirc \square = \square$$

How many leaves are there altogether?

$$\square + \square + \square = \square$$

How many fruits are left?

$$\square - \square - \square = \square$$

Chapter 3   Numbers up to 20 and their addition and subtraction

3.1   Numbers 11 – 20

 Learning objective

Read and write numbers to 20

 Basic questions

① Look at the pictures and write the numbers in the boxes.

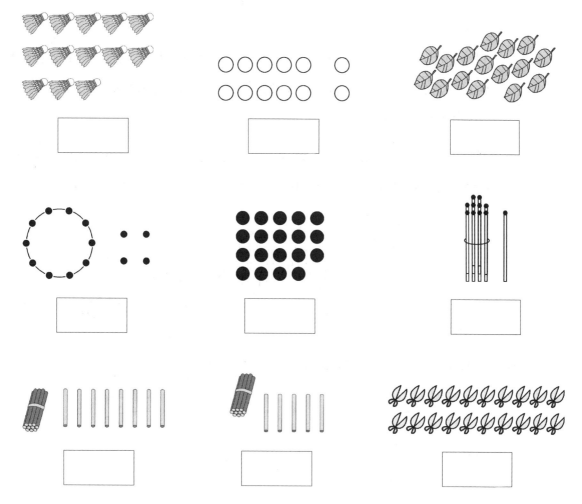

2 Fill in with numbers.

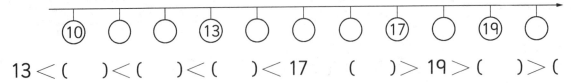

13 < ( ) < ( ) < ( ) < 17   ( ) > 19 > ( ) > (

3 Find patterns and fill in with numbers.

16	14			6

20	15			0

19 17 ◯ ◯ ◯ 9 ◯ ◯ ◯ ◯

Challenge and extension question

4 Hop on numbers.

(a) The little puppy hops on odd numbers (11, 13, ⋯). Help the puppy draw a green line to link the numbers from the least to the greatest.

The little chick hops on even numbers (10, 12, ⋯). Help the chick draw a red line to link the number from the greatest to the least.

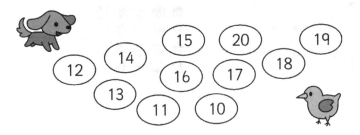

(b) Write down the above numbers below.

Odd numbers   Even numbers

3.2   Tens and ones

Partition numbers into tens and ones

 Basic questions

1 Count and draw a line to match.

| 14 | | 12 | | 15 | | 11 |

2 Split numbers into tens and ones. The first one has been done for you.

14
10+4

○○○○○○○○○○
●●●
13
10+

○○○○○○○○○○
●●●●●●

○○○○○○○○○○
●●●●●●●●

○○○○○○○○○○
●●●●●●●●●●

○○○○○○○○○○
●●●●●●●

❸ Look at the pictures and write the numbers sentences.

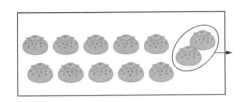

□ ○ □ = □

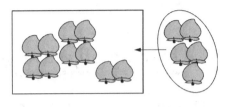

□ ○ □ = □

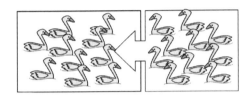

□ ○ □ = □

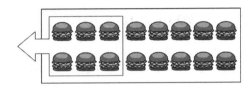

□ ○ □ = □

4 Write the numbers in the boxes.

$10 + 2 = \square$ $10 + 5 = \square$ $10 + 9 = \square$

$2 + 10 = \square$ $5 + 10 = \square$ $9 + 10 = \square$

$18 = 10 + \square$ $16 = 10 + \square$ $13 = 10 + \square$

$20 = \square + 10$ $19 = \square + 9$ $15 = 5 + \square$

Challenge and extension question

❺ Write the numbers in the boxes.

$10 + \square = 14$ $10 + \square = 17$

$\square + 1 = 11$ $\square + 8 = 18$

$6 + \square = 16$ $\square + 10 = 20$

$12 - \square = 10$ $16 - \square = 10$

3.3 Ordering numbers up to 20

Compare and order numbers to 20

Basic questions

1 Write the numbers in the circles.

①②○○⑤○⑦○○⑩⑪○⑬○○⑯○⑱○○

2 Count and then colour accordingly.

●②●④●○⑥⑦⑧⑨⑩⑪⑫⑬⑭⑮⑯⑰⑱⑲⑳

①●③●⑤●⑦⑧⑨⑩⑪⑫⑬⑭⑮⑯⑰⑱⑲⑳

①②③④○⑥⑦⑧⑨○⑪⑫⑬⑭⑮⑯⑰⑱⑲⑳

3 Fill in the numbers properly.

☐ 11 ☐ ☐ 14 ☐ ☐ ☐ 18 ☐ ☐

(a) The two numbers before and after 15 are ____ and ____.

(b) The number after 18 is ____ and the number before 11 is ____.

(c) The number between 11 and 13 is _____ .

(d) The numbers greater than 12 but less than 18 are _____ .

(e) The numbers less than 20 but greater than 15 are _____ .

4 Swap the positions of two numbers in each set so the new order of the numbers forms a pattern. The first one is an example.

(a) 1, 3, 9, 7, 5   New: 1, 3, 5, 7, 9

(b) 20, 19, 18, 17, 15, 16   New: _____

(c) 3, 6, 5, 4, 7   New: _____

(d) 4, 12, 8, 16, 20   New: _____

5 Find out and then circle the number in each set below so the remaining numbers forms a pattern. The first one is an example.

(a) 3, 5, 7, 8, 9   Remaining: 3, 5, 7, 9

(b) 2, 4, 6, 8, 9   Remaining: _____

(c) 18, 17, 15, 13, 11   Remaining: _____

(d) 6, 9, 12, 13, 15, 18   Remaining: _____

Challenge and extension question

6 (a) A number is greater than 12 but less than 15. The number could be _____ .

(b) A number is less than 20 but greater than 16. The number could be _____ .

(c) Add some numbers before and after 9 to make a number pattern.

_____ , _____ , _____ , 9, _____ , _____ , _____ .

3.4 Addition and subtraction (I)

 Learning objective

Add and subtract using number bonds to 20

Basic questions

1 Look at the diagrams and write the number sentences.

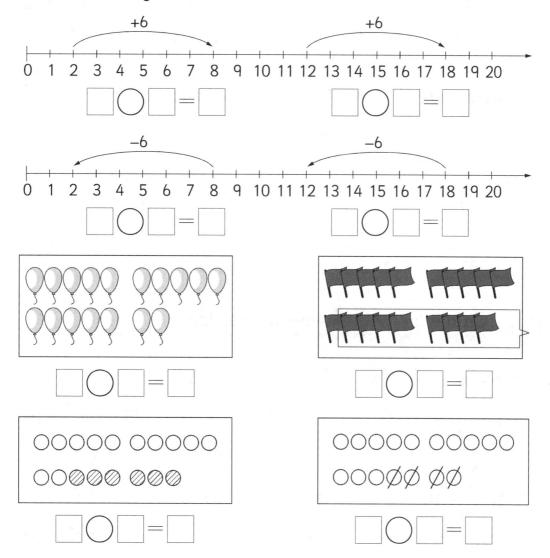

```
        +6                              +6
   ┌───────────┐                  ┌───────────┐
───┼─┼─┼─┼─┼─┼─┼─┼─┼─┼─┼─┼─┼─┼─┼─┼─┼─┼─┼─┼──►
   0 1 2 3 4 5 6 7 8 9 10 11 12 13 14 15 16 17 18 19 20
```

□ ○ □ = □   □ ○ □ = □

```
        −6                              −6
   ┌───────────┐                  ┌───────────┐
───┼─┼─┼─┼─┼─┼─┼─┼─┼─┼─┼─┼─┼─┼─┼─┼─┼─┼─┼─┼──►
   0 1 2 3 4 5 6 7 8 9 10 11 12 13 14 15 16 17 18 19 20
```

□ ○ □ = □   □ ○ □ = □

□ ○ □ = □   □ ○ □ = □

□ ○ □ = □   □ ○ □ = □

2 Work out the sums.

$6 + 2 =$	$3 + 5 =$	$4 + 4 =$	$5 + 2 =$
$16 + 2 =$	$13 + 5 =$	$14 + 4 =$	$15 + 2 =$
$1 + 5 =$	$6 + 3 =$	$3 + 3 =$	$2 + 4 =$
$11 + 5 =$	$16 + 3 =$	$13 + 3 =$	$12 + 4 =$

3 Calculate.

$6 - 2 =$	$7 - 5 =$	$4 - 3 =$	$5 - 2 =$
$16 - 2 =$	$17 - 5 =$	$14 - 3 =$	$15 - 2 =$
$9 - 5 =$	$6 - 4 =$	$8 - 3 =$	$9 - 4 =$
$19 - 5 =$	$16 - 4 =$	$18 - 3 =$	$19 - 4 =$

4 Think carefully and then fill in the boxes.

$3 + 5 = \square$	$5 + 3 = \square$	$2 + 7 = \square$
$13 + 5 = \square$	$\square + \square = \square$	$\square + \square = \square$
$4 - 2 = \square$	$6 - 5 = \square$	$7 - 2 = \square$
$14 - 2 = \square$	$\square - \square = \square$	$\square - \square = \square$

Challenge and extension question

5 Fill in the $\bigcirc$ with ">", "<" or "=".

$15 \bigcirc 2 + 13$	$16 - 2 \bigcirc 16$	$15 + 2 \bigcirc 15 - 2$
$13 \bigcirc 12 + 4$	$17 - 5 \bigcirc 10$	$19 - 5 \bigcirc 11 + 3$
$14 \bigcirc 19 - 4$	$13 + 7 \bigcirc 20$	$17 - 4 \bigcirc 17 - 3$
$16 \bigcirc 20 - 10$	$14 + 6 \bigcirc 18$	$2 + 16 \bigcirc 12 + 6$

3.5 Addition and subtraction (II) (1)

 Learning objective

Add numbers to 20, crossing the ten and partitioning

Basic questions

1. Colour the dots and work out the sums. The first one has been done for you.

⊘⊘⊘⊘⊘ ⊘⊘⊘⊘●
●●○○○ ○○○○○

$9 + 3 = 12$

⊘⊘⊘⊘⊘ ⊘⊘⊘○○
○○○○○ ○○○○○

$8 + 6 = \square$

○○○○○ ○○○○○
○○○○○ ○○○○○

$7 + 5 = \square$

○○○○○ ○○○○○
○○○○○ ○○○○○

$6 + 6 = \square$

2. Do addition using a number line.

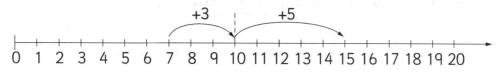

$7 + 8 = \square$

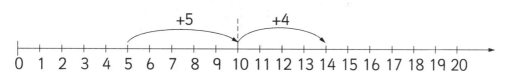

$5 + 9 = \square$

③ Fill in the missing numbers.

9 + 3 = ☐

10

8 + 5 = ☐

10

6 + 9 = ☐

10

8 + 4 = ☐

10

9 + 9 = ☐

10

7 + 9 = ☐

10

④ Fill in the missing numbers.

8 + 5 = ☐

Step I: 8 + 2 = ☐

Step II: 10 + 3 = ☐

4 + 9 = ☐

Step I: 4 + 6 = ☐

Step II: 10 + 3 = ☐

7 + 7 = ☐

Step I: 7 + 3 = ☐

Step II: 10 + 4 = ☐

9 + 5 = ☐

Step I: 9 + ☐ = ☐

Step II: 10 + ☐ = ☐

 Challenge and extension question

⑤ Look at the picture and write addition sentences.

By size:

_____

_____

By shape:

_____

_____

3.6 Addition and subtraction (II) (2)

 Learning objective

Add using number bonds to 20 and the commutative law

 Basic questions

1 Look at the pictures and write the number sentences.

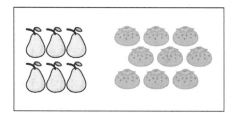

6+☐=☐

9+☐=☐

8+☐=☐

☐+☐=☐

☐+☐=☐

☐+☐=☐

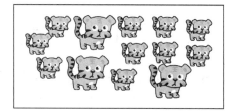

☐+☐=☐

☐+☐=☐

7 books are inside.

How many books are in total?

☐○☐=☐

9 pens are inside.

How many pens are in total?

☐○☐=☐

2 Fill in the table.

Addend	8	9	5	9	3	6
Addend	5	4	7	8	8	5
Sum						

3 Work out the sums.

$9+2=$	$8+3=$	$7+5=$	$4+9=$
$9+3=$	$8+4=$	$7+6=$	$3+8=$
$9+4=$	$8+5=$	$7+7=$	$3+9=$
$9+5=$	$8+6=$	$7+8=$	$2+9=$
$9+6=$	$8+7=$	$7+9=$	$1+13=$
$9+7=$	$8+8=$	$6+5=$	$2+17=$
$9+8=$	$8+9=$	$6+6=$	$15+3=$
$9+9=$	$7+4=$	$6+7=$	$14+6=$

4 Fill in the ◯ with ">", "<" or "=".

$7+8$ ◯ 13 $4+9$ ◯ 17 20 ◯ $13+7$ 16 ◯ $7+5$

$5+9$ ◯ 13 $8+7$ ◯ 15 14 ◯ $8+4$ 19 ◯ $9+9$

$6+8$ ◯ $6+9$ $5+8$ ◯ $9+4$ $7+7$ ◯ $10+4$

Challenge and extension question

5 Write the missing numbers.

$\square - 3 = 7$ $\square - 6 = 9$ $\square - 9 = 5$ $\square - 8 = 4$

$\square - 7 = 5$ $\square - 9 = 8$ $\square - 6 = 6$ $\square - 7 = 9$

3.7 Addition and subtraction (II) (3)

 Learning objective

Subtract within 20, crossing the ten and partitioning

Basic questions

1 Cross out the circles and then complete the subtractions.

⊘⊘⊘⊘⊘ ⊘⊘⊘⊘⊘
⊘⊘⊘⊘⊘ ○○○○○

$15 - 7 = \boxed{}$

⊘⊘⊘⊘⊘ ⊘⊘⊘⊘⊘
⊘⊘○○○ ○○○○○

$12 - 5 = \boxed{}$

⊘⊘⊘⊘⊘ ⊘⊘⊘⊘⊘
⊘⊘⊘⊘○ ○○○○○

$14 - 6 = \boxed{}$

⊘⊘⊘⊘⊘ ⊘⊘⊘⊘⊘
⊘⊘⊘⊘⊘ ⊘○○○○

$16 - 9 = \boxed{}$

2 Do subtraction using a number line.

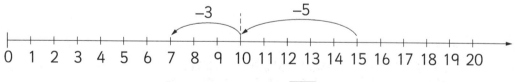

$15 - 8 = \boxed{}$

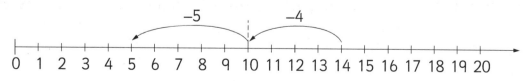

$14 - 9 = \boxed{}$

3 Fill in the missing numbers.

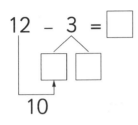

12 – 3 = ☐
☐ ☐
10

11 – 6 = ☐
☐ ☐
10

13 – 5 = ☐
☐ ☐
10

16 – 8 = ☐
☐ ☐
10

17 – 9 = ☐
☐ ☐
10

14 – 6 = ☐
☐ ☐
10

4 Fill in the missing numbers.

$14 - 5 =$ ☐

Step I: $14 - 4 =$ ☐

Step II: $10 - 1 =$ ☐

$12 - 9 =$ ☐

Step I: $12 - 2 =$ ☐

Step II: $10 - 7 =$ ☐

$15 - 7 =$ ☐

Step I: $15 - 5 =$ ☐

Step II: $10 - 2 =$ ☐

$11 - 9 =$ ☐

Step I: $11 - 1 =$ ☐

Step II: $10 - $ ☐ $ = $ ☐

 Challenge and extension question

5 Fill in the ◯ so the sum of the numbers on each line is 20.

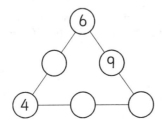

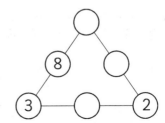

3.8　Addition and subtraction (II) (4)

 Learning objective

Subtract numbers within 20

 Basic questions

1 Look at the pictures and write the number sentences.

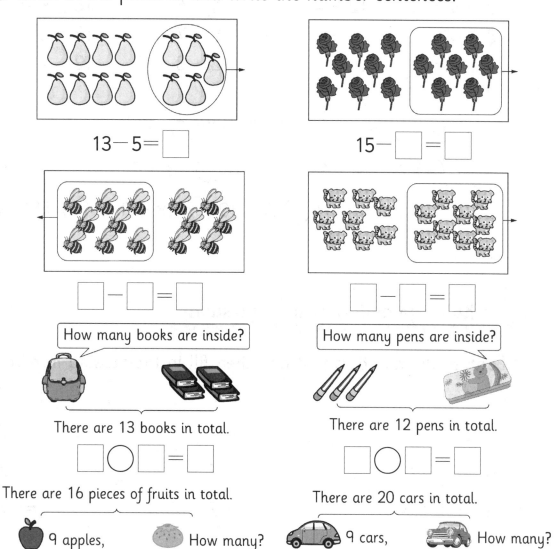

$13 - 5 = \boxed{}$

$15 - \boxed{} = \boxed{}$

$\boxed{} - \boxed{} = \boxed{}$

$\boxed{} - \boxed{} = \boxed{}$

How many books are inside?

How many pens are inside?

There are 13 books in total.

$\boxed{} \bigcirc \boxed{} = \boxed{}$

There are 12 pens in total.

$\boxed{} \bigcirc \boxed{} = \boxed{}$

There are 16 pieces of fruits in total.

9 apples,　How many?

$\boxed{} \bigcirc \boxed{} = \boxed{}$

There are 20 cars in total.

9 cars,　How many?

$\boxed{} \bigcirc \boxed{} = \boxed{}$

2 Fill in the table.

Minuend	11	13	15	16	12	14
Subtrahend	5	4	7	8	9	6
Difference						

3 Calculate.

$11 - 2 =$	$11 - 8 =$	$12 - 5 =$	$13 - 8 =$
$12 - 3 =$	$12 - 4 =$	$14 - 6 =$	$16 - 9 =$
$13 - 4 =$	$12 - 6 =$	$15 - 7 =$	$13 - 6 =$
$14 - 5 =$	$14 - 7 =$	$12 - 8 =$	$12 - 7 =$

4 Fill in the ◯ with ">", "<" or "=".

$13 - 8 \bigcirc 7$ $14 - 9 \bigcirc 7$ $6 \bigcirc 13 - 7$ $9 \bigcirc 14 - 6$

$14 - 5 \bigcirc 8$ $16 - 9 \bigcirc 5$ $10 \bigcirc 18 - 9$ $7 \bigcirc 11 - 9$

Challenge and extension question

5 Look at the numbers first and then fill in the missing numbers.

$8 - 1 = 7$ $\square - \square = 7$ $\square - \square = 7$

$9 - 2 = 7$ $\square - \square = 7$ $\square - \square = 7$

$10 - 3 = 7$ $\square - \square = 7$ $\square - \square = 7$

$\square - \square = 7$ $\square - \square = 7$ $\square - \square = 7$

3.9 Addition and subtraction (II) (5)

 Learning objective

Add and subtract numbers to 20

 Basic questions

1 Look at the pictures and write the number sentences.

7   5

How many rabbits are there in total?

☐ ◯ ☐ = ☐

How many are in the basket?

There are 11 carrots in total.

☐ ◯ ☐ = ☐

How many are inside?

There are 13 peaches in total.

☐ ◯ ☐ = ☐

☐ ◯ ☐ = ☐

9 people are on the bus.

How many people are there in total?

☐ ◯ ☐ = ☐

4 cans were drunk.

How many cans were there at first?

☐ ◯ ☐ = ☐

How many are left?

☐ ◯ ☐ = ☐

There were 12 rabbits at first.

☐ ◯ ☐ = ☐

2 Calculate.

$12 - 0 =$	$5 + 7 =$	$15 - 8 =$	$13 - 5 =$
$9 + 6 =$	$11 - 3 =$	$9 + 5 =$	$12 - 4 =$
$7 + 6 =$	$14 - 7 =$	$13 - 8 =$	$19 + 1 =$

3 Calculate and then draw lines to match the results.

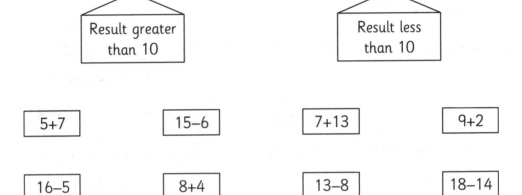

4 Fill in the boxes.

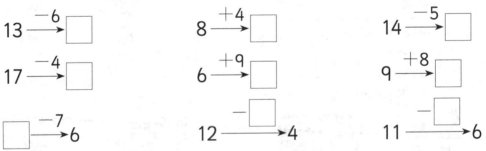

Challenge and extension question

5 Choose six of the seven numbers: 3, 4, 5, 6, 7, 8 and 9. Use them to fill in the brackets so that the equations are true.

$(\quad) + (\quad) = (\quad) + (\quad) = (\quad) + (\quad)$

3.10 Let's talk and calculate (III)

 Learning objective

Interpret word problems using addition and subtraction facts to 20

 Basic questions

① Read the following and write the addition or subtraction sentences.

There were 16 🍎 on the plate.	There were 12 🍐 on the table.
7 🍎 were eaten.	9 🍐 were taken away.
How many 🍎 were left?	How many 🍐 are left on the table?

☐ ○ ☐ = ☐   ☐ ○ ☐ = ☐

6 🐦 were in the tree.	9 🚗 were in the car park.
Another 5 🐦 arrived.	Another 7 🚗 drove into the car park.
How many 🐦 are in the tree now?	How many 🚗 are in the car park now?

☐ ○ ☐ = ☐   ☐ ○ ☐ = ☐

There are 6 🏀.	There are 7 ▨.
There are 14 ⚽.	There are 5 ⌓.
How many more 🏀 are needed to be as many as ⚽?	How many ▨ and ⌓ are there in total?

☐ ○ ☐ = ☐   ☐ ○ ☐ = ☐

2 Read the problems and then write the number sentences.

(a) There were 6 chicks playing on the grass field. Another 7 chicks joined them. How many chicks are there now?

Number sentence: _____

(b) Tom has 6 yellow pencils. He has as many blue pencils as yellow pencils. How many pencils does he have altogether?

Number sentence: _____

(c) Mary's father bought 12 pears. She ate 3 of them. How many pears were left?

Number sentence: _____

(d) 7 library books were borrowed out. Later another 9 books were borrowed out. How many library books were borrowed out in total?

Number sentence: _____

(e) John needs to make 12 flags. He has made 8. How many more flags does he need to make?

Number sentence: _____

(f) There are 9 oranges left after Tom and John ate 6 oranges. How many oranges were there at first?

Number sentence: _____

Challenge and extension question

3 Add a condition to complete the story. Then write the number sentences and find the answers.

(a) There are 8 English books. _____. How many English books and mathematics books are there altogether? Number sentence: _____

(b) _____. 9 cars drove away. How many cars are left? Number sentence: _____

3.11 Adding on and taking away

Learning objective

Use the inverse relationship between addition and subtraction with numbers to 20

Basic questions

1 Look at the pictures and fill in the boxes.

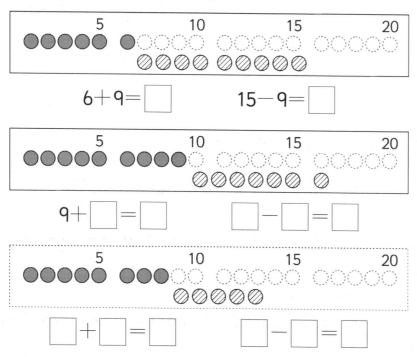

6+9=☐   15−9=☐

9+☐=☐   ☐−☐=☐

☐+☐=☐   ☐−☐=☐

2 Look at the pictures. Write the addition and subtraction sentences.

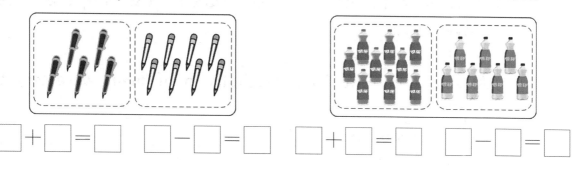

☐+☐=☐   ☐−☐=☐   ☐+☐=☐   ☐−☐=☐

3 Fill in the ☐ with numbers and the ◯ with " + " or "—".

15 ⟨ +3 / −3 ⟩ ☐   17 ⟨ +2 / −☐ ⟩ ☐   9 ⟨ ◯☐ / −9 ⟩ 18   14 ⟨ +5 / ◯☐ ⟩ ☐

13 ⟨ ◯☐ / ◯☐ ⟩ 14   7 ⟨ ◯☐ / ◯☐ ⟩ 15   8 ⟨ +4 / −4 ⟩ ☐   7 ⟨ +5 / ◯☐ ⟩ ☐

4 Think carefully and then fill in the boxes.

$16 + 2 = \square$ $\square + 4 = \square$ $18 - 9 = \square$

$18 - 2 = \square$ $14 - 4 = \square$ $\square + 9 = \square$

$7 + 4 = \square$ $16 - 8 = \square$ $13 - 4 = \square$

$11 - \square = \square$ $\square + 8 = \square$ $\square + \square = \square$

Challenge and extension question

5 Read each number story and write the question. Then write the number sentence.

(a) There were 18 children on the train. 4 of them got off at a station. _____?

Number sentence: _____

(b) John's father first bought 15 books, and then bought another 4 books. _____?

Number sentence: _____

(c) There were 14 cars in the car park at first. 8 of them then drove away. _____?

Number sentence: _____

(d) A school bought 13 basketballs. 5 of them were lent to pupils. _____?

Number sentence: _____

3.12 Number walls

 ## Learning objective

Use number bonds to 20

 ## Basic questions

1 Fill in the number walls. The first one has been done for you.

```
        6
    3       3
  2    1    2
```

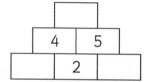

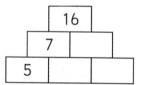

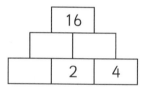

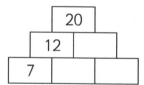

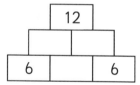

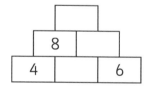

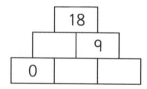

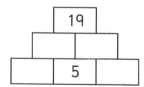

2 Fill in the number walls.

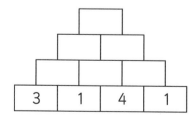

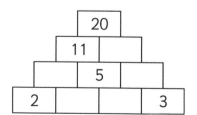

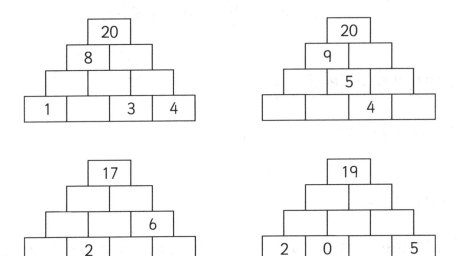

 Challenge and extension question

3 Create your own number walls.

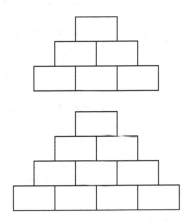

Chapter 4   Recognising shapes

4.1   Shapes of objects (1)

 Learning objective

Recognise and name 3-D shapes

 Basic questions

1 Draw lines to match the solid figures with the shapes below.

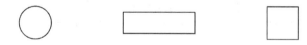

2 Count and then fill the numbers in the brackets.

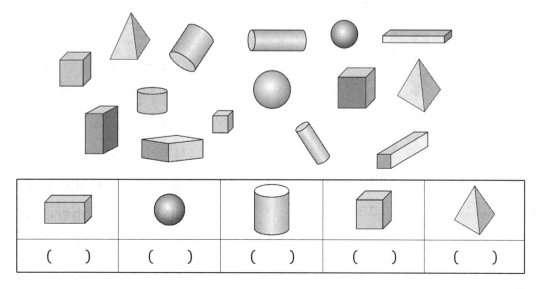

3 Try it out and then fill in the table.

	Can't roll	Can roll	
		in one direction	in all directions
	✓		

Challenge and extension question

4 Count and then fill the numbers in the blanks.

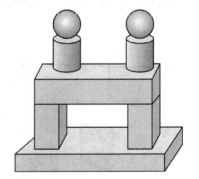

Cube(s): _____   Cylinder(s): _____

Cuboid(s): _____   Pyramid(s): _____

Cube(s): _____   Cylinder(s): _____

Cuboid(s): _____   Sphere(s): _____

4.2   Shapes of objects (2)

 Learning objective

Recognise and name 3-D shapes

Basic questions

1. Draw lines to link the objects with the shapes in the middle. The first one has been done for you.

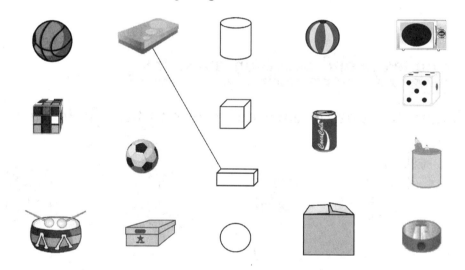

2. Count the shapes and fill the number in the brackets.

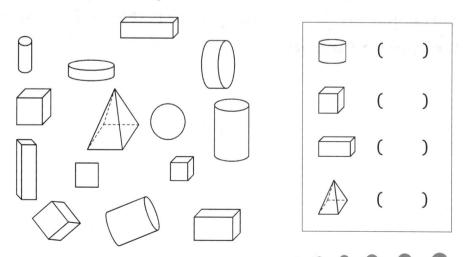

3 Draw lines to match each object to the correct shape in the grid below.

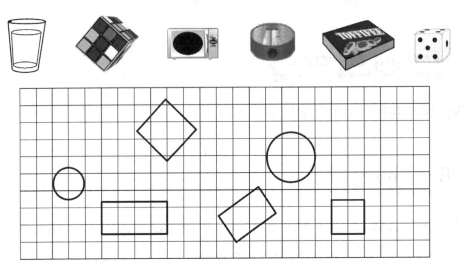

 Challenge and extension questions

4 Count the cubes in each diagram and then fill in the (   ).

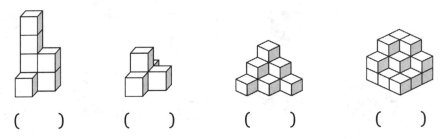

(   )   (   )   (   )   (   )

5 Think carefully and then rearrange the sticks.
3 triangles are formed using 9 sticks. Move 3 of the sticks so they form 5 triangles.

Unit test 4

1 Complete the mental sums.

$5+2=$	$3+7=$	$14-6=$
$(\quad)+6=10$	$4+2=$	$18-6=$
$17-3=$	$15=(\quad)+4$	$9-3=$
$4+6=$	$9+8=$	$6=(\quad)-2$
$15+2=$	$10+7=$	$14+4=$
$(\quad)-3=9$	$7-3=$	$5+7=$
$7+7=$	$7+(\quad)=13-(\quad)$	

2 Count and then compare.

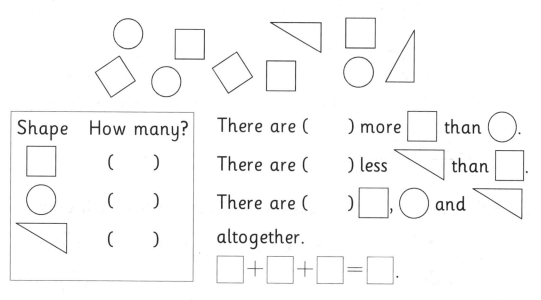

Shape	How many?
▢	( )
◯	( )
◺	( )

There are (   ) more ▢ than ◯.

There are (   ) less ◺ than ▢.

There are (   ) ▢, ◯ and ◺

altogether.

▢ + ▢ + ▢ = ▢.

❸ Count and then fill in each bracket with the number of the object.

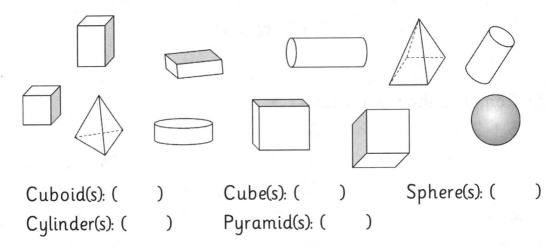

Cuboid(s): (   )   Cube(s): (   )   Sphere(s): (   )

Cylinder(s): (   )   Pyramid(s): (   )

④ Fill in the number walls.

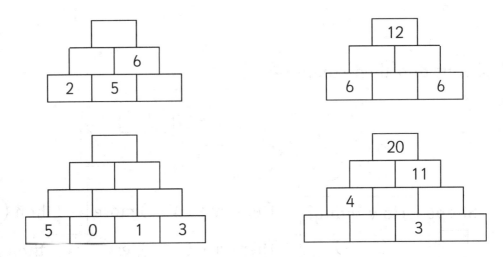

❺ Fill in the (   ) with the correct number for each object.

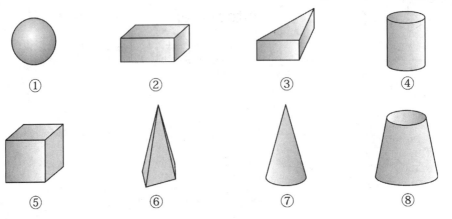

① ② ③ ④

⑤ ⑥ ⑦ ⑧

(a) The object(s) having the shape of ▭: (   ).

(b) The object(s) having the shape of ☐: (   ).

(c) The object(s) having the shape of △: (   ).

(d) The object(s) having the shape of ○: (   ).

6 Look at the diagrams and write the number sentences.

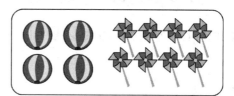

9+☐=☐

15−☐=☐

☐+☐=☐

☐−☐=☐

7 Count and then fill in the brackets.

(a) 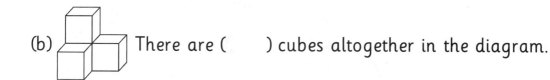 There are (   ) rectangles altogether in the diagram.

(b) There are (   ) cubes altogether in the diagram.

Chapter 5 Consolidation and enhancement

5.1 Sorting shapes

 Learning objective

Recognise and sort 2-D shapes

 Basic questions

1 Count and write the numbers in the brackets.

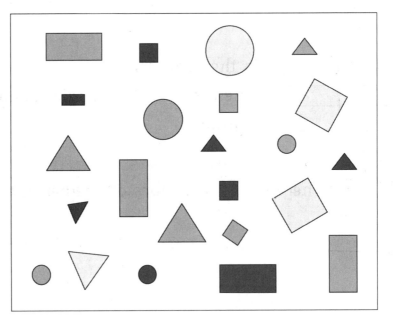

(a) Sort by shape.

   ☐   ▭   ◯   △

  (   )   (   )   (   )   (   )

(b) Sort by size.

          Big   Small

        (   )   (   )

2 Sort the shapes in different ways and then put the numbers into the ovals below.

(a) Sort by _____ .

（oval）（oval）（oval）（oval）

(b) Sort by _____ .

（oval）（oval）

 Challenge and extension question

3 Fill in the blanks.

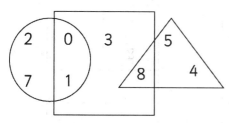

The numbers in the ○ are _____ .

The numbers in the □ are _____ .

The numbers in both ○ and □ are

_____ .

The number in both △ and □ is

_____ .

99

5.2 Calculating with reasoning

 Learning objective

Add and subtract numbers to 20

 Basic questions

1 Fill in the boxes.

8 + 4 = (   )   8 + 5 = (   )   8 + (   ) = (   )

12 − 8 = (   )   (   ) − 8 = (   )   14 − (   ) = (   )

12 − 4 = (   )   13 − (   ) = (   )   (   ) − (   ) = (   )

2 Think carefully and then fill in the space provided.

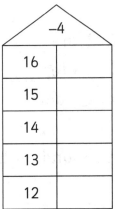

+6	
10	
11	
12	
13	
14	

+7	
10	
9	
8	

8+	
4	
5	
6	

−4	
16	
15	
14	
13	
12	

−6	
11	
12	
13	

15−	
9	
8	
7	

3 Calculate.

8 + 4 =	10 + 8 =	7 + 5 =
8 + 5 =	11 + 8 =	8 + 6 =
9 + 5 =	11 + 9 =	9 + 7 =
18 − 8 =	16 − 7 =	12 − 6 =
18 − 9 =	15 − 7 =	13 − 7 =
18 − 10 =	14 − 7 =	14 − 8 =

4 Fill in the brackets with suitable numbers. (Think about the relationships between the numbers in the number sentences.)

5 + 2 = (   )   8 − 6 = (   )

15 + 2 = (   )   18 − 6 = (   )

25 + (   ) = (   )   28 − (   ) = (   )

35 + (   ) = (   )   38 − (   ) = (   )

Challenge and extension question

5 What number does each figure stand for?

△	○	□	19
△	△	△	15
♡	☺	△	14
12	20	16	

△ = (   )   ♡ = (   )

□ = (   )   ○ = (   )

☺ = (   )

5.3 Comparing numbers

 Learning objective

Compare numbers to 20

Basic questions

1 Think carefully and then draw.

(a) ☆ ☆ ☆ ☆ ☆

_____ (Draw as many □ as ☆.)

(b) △ △ △

_____ (Draw one more □ than △.)

(c) ○ ○ ○ ○

_____ (Draw one fewer □ than ○.)

(d) ♡ ♡ ♡ ♡

_____ (Draw 2 more △ than ♡.)

(e) ☺ ☺ ☺ ☺ ☺ ☺

_____ (Draw 3 fewer ○ than ☺.)

2 Compare and then fill in the ◯ with ">", "<" or "=".

(a) 6 ◯ 8   12 ◯ 9   15 ◯ 20

   18 ◯ 8   16 ◯ 14   1 ◯ 0

(b) 9 + 6 ◯ 17   16 − 5 ◯ 9   15 ◯ 20 − 5

   12 + 8 ◯ 18   15 − 6 ◯ 11   17 ◯ 7 + 7

(c) 7 + 9 ◯ 19 − 2   18 − 3 ◯ 18 − 2   20 − 6 ◯ 8 + 8

$8 + 7 \bigcirc 6 + 9 \qquad 20 - 4 \bigcirc 11 + 5 \qquad 5 + 9 \bigcirc 17 - 5$

❸ Fill in the boxes with suitable numbers.

(a) $18 > \square \qquad 10 < \square \qquad 7 > \square$

$5 < \square < \square < 10 \qquad 18 > \square > 16 > \square$

(b) $8 + \square < 14 \qquad \square - 10 < 3 \qquad \square > 16 - 5$

$20 - \square > 10 \qquad \square + 4 > 12 \qquad 11 < \square + 6$

(c) $\square + 4 < 20 - 4 \qquad \square - 6 > 4 + 4 \qquad 10 - 7 > \square - 8$

$16 - \square < 7 + 7 \qquad 3 + 8 < \square - 5 \qquad 6 + 7 < 9 + \square$

Challenge and extension questions

4 Without calculation, fill in the $\bigcirc$ with ">", "<" or "=".

$24 + 6 \bigcirc 24 + 8 \qquad 55 + 9 \bigcirc 54 + 9 \qquad 35 + 7 \bigcirc 33 + 9$

$48 - 5 \bigcirc 48 - 8 \qquad 66 - 9 \bigcirc 56 - 9 \qquad 55 - 7 \bigcirc 54 - 6$

❺ What is the greatest number you can fill in each box?

$7 + \square < 15 \qquad 18 > \square + 9 \qquad 8 + \square < 20 - 8$

$\square - 6 < 5 \qquad 7 < 13 - \square \qquad 20 - \square > 6 + 6$

5.4 Half and quarter

 Learning objective

Recognise a half and a quarter of shapes and quantities

 Basic questions

1 Has each shape been halved? (put "✓" for yes and "✕" for no.)

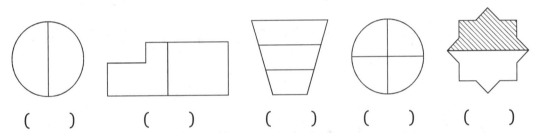

( )   ( )   ( )   ( )   ( )

2 Write half or quarter to represent the shaded part of the diagram.

(a)   (b)   (c)   (d)

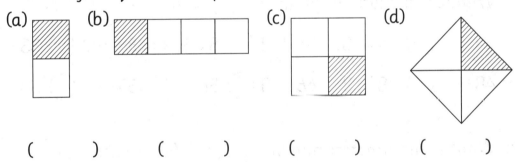

( )   ( )   ( )   ( )

3 Colour each of the following as indicated.

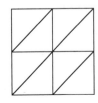   

A half   A quarter   The whole

4 Halve each group of dots and then write the number sentences.

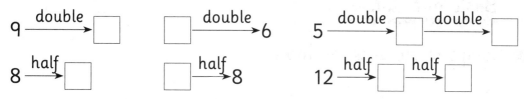

□ = □ + □   □ = □ + □   □ = □ + □

5 Fill in the boxes.

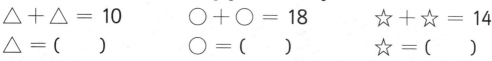

9 —double→ □   □ —double→ 6   5 —double→ □ —double→ □

8 —half→ □   □ —half→ 8   12 —half→ □ —half→ □

6 What number does each figure stand for?

$\triangle + \triangle = 10$ $\bigcirc + \bigcirc = 18$ $\star + \star = 14$

$\triangle = ($ $)$ $\bigcirc = ($ $)$ $\star = ($ $)$

 Challenge and extension questions

7 Think carefully and then fill in the (   ).

🍉 = (   ) 🍎

8 John had 20 marbles at first. He gave half of them to Amy and a quarter of them to Ruth.

(a) How many marbles did Amy receive? (   )

(b) How many marbles did Ruth receive? (   )

(c) How many marbles did John still have? (   )

5.5 Let's do additions together

 Learning objective

Use number bonds to 20

 Basic questions

1 Complete the addition table.

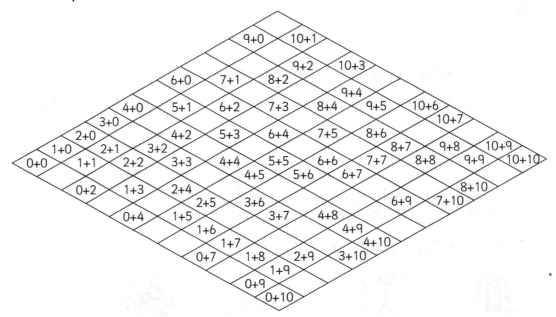

2 Use the same colour to colour the additions with the answers of 4, 7, 10, 13, 16 in the above table.

3 Look at the table above and complete the following.

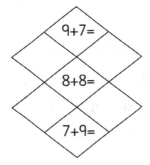

9+7=

8+8=

7+9=

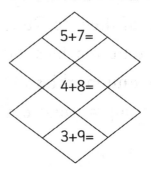

5+7=

4+8=

3+9=

4 Fill in the numbers on each floor of the houses.

13
3+10
4+9
5+8
+
+
+
+
+

18
8+10
+
+
+
+
+
+
+

10
0+10
+
+
+
+
+
+
+

15
+
+
+
+
+
+
+
+

5 Make up addition problems and write the number sentences.

(a) There were 10 birds in the tree. Another 8 birds joined them.

_____ ?

Number sentence: _____

(b) There are 12 girls and 8 boys in a choir.

_____ ?

Number sentence: _____

(c) After 9 cars drove away, there were 6 cars left in the car park._____ ?

Number sentence: _____

Challenge and extension question

6 Fill in the ◯ with numbers 1, 2, 3, 4, 5, 6 and 7 so that the sum of the three numbers on each line is 16.

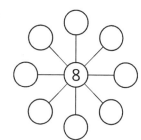

5.6 Let's do subtractions together

 Learning objective

Use number bonds to subtract numbers within 20

 Basic questions

1 Complete the subtraction table.

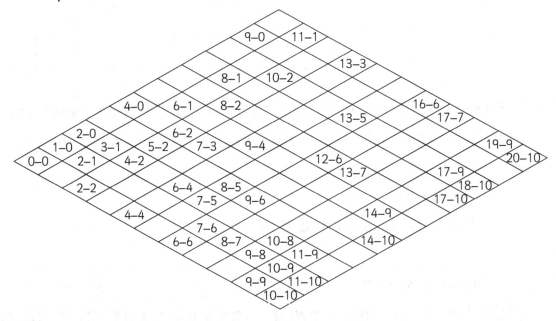

2 Use the same colour to colour the subtractions with the answers of 0, 3, 6 and 9 in the above table.

3 Look at the table above and complete the following.

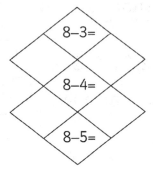

8–3=

8–4=

8–5=

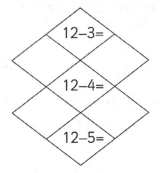

12–3=

12–4=

12–5=

4 Fill in the numbers on each floor of the houses.

12
13–1
14–2
15–3
–
–
–
–

8
10–2
11–
–
–
–
–
–

10
20–10
19–
–
–
–
–
–

5
10–5
11–
–
–
–
–
–

5 Make up a subtraction problem for each question.

(a) Mary's mum bought 20 apples. They ate 8 of them.

_____?

Number sentence: _____

(b) There are 15 white rabbits and black rabbits in total. 8 of them are white rabbits. _____?

Number sentence: _____

(c) There are 12 basketballs and 9 volleyballs in the sports room. _____?

Number sentence: _____

Challenge and extension question

6 Fill in the ( ) using the eight numbers 5, 6, 7, 8, 9, 10, 11 and 12. Each number should be used only once.

(a) ( )−( )=( )−( )=( )−( )=( )−( )

(b) ( )−( )=( )−( )=( )−( )=( )−( )

5.7 Making number sentences

 Learning objective

Make addition and subtraction sentences using the inverse relationship

 Basic questions

1 Look at the pictures and write the number sentences.

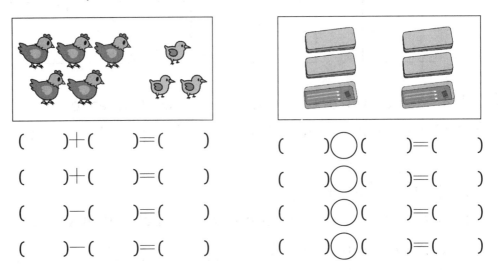

( )+( )=( )
( )+( )=( )
( )−( )=( )
( )−( )=( )

( )◯( )=( )
( )◯( )=( )
( )◯( )=( )
( )◯( )=( )

2 In each group, calculate first and then fill in the brackets with the three numbers given in the completed calculation.

9+6=
( )+( )=( )
( )−( )=( )
( )−( )=( )

12+8=
( )+( )=( )
( )−( )=( )
( )−( )=( )

16−9=
( )+( )=( )
( )+( )=( )
( )−( )=( )

20−6=
( )+( )=( )
( )+( )=( )
( )−( )=( )

3 Use the three numbers given in each group to make two addition sentences and two subtraction sentences.

     7 8 15   5 20 15   9 9 0

_____   _____   _____

_____   _____   _____

_____   _____   _____

_____   _____   _____

4 Choose 3 numbers in each group. Then make two addition sentences and two subtraction sentences.

     4 6 8 12   5 9 12 14

_____   _____

_____   _____

_____   _____

_____   _____

Challenge and extension question

5 Put the 9 numbers below into 3 groups. Then use the 3 numbers in each group to make two addition sentences and two subtraction sentences.

2, 6, 7, 8, 9, 10, 12, 14, 16

_____   _____   _____

_____   _____   _____

_____   _____   _____

_____   _____   _____

5.8 Mathematics playground (1)

 Learning objective

Read, write, add and subtract numbers to 20

 Basic questions

1 Work out these mentally. Write the answers.

$3+5=$	$10-7=$	$6+4=$	$5+4+6=$
$9+0=$	$8-6=$	$7+8=$	$8+9-5=$
$13+2=$	$19-9=$	$11-6=$	$18-5-7=$
$7+7=$	$14-5=$	$17-0=$	$16-6+5=$
$8-8=$	$12-3=$	$9+9=$	$6+6+6=$

2 Fill in the blanks.

(a)

8			12		15				

	2	4		10	14			

19	17				7			

(b) 6 ones and 1 ten make _____ . 2 tens make _____ .

There are _____ ten and _____ ones in 18. There are

_____ fives in 20.

(c)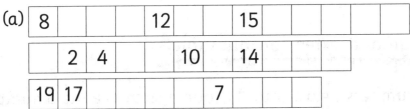

(d) Fill in with the numbers before or after the number.

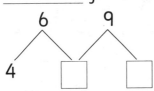 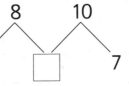 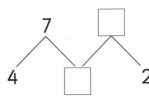

112

3 Look at the pictures and write the number sentences.

(a)

(   )+(   )=(   )

(   )+(   )=(   )

(   )−(   )=(   )

(   )−(   )=(   )

(b)
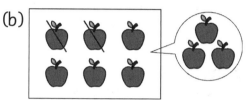

(   )◯(   )◯(   )

=(   )

(c)

(   )◯(   )◯(   )

=(   )

4 Fill in the ◯ with ">", "<" or "=".

7 ◯ 9   8+8 ◯ 15   12 ◯ 20−6   7+4 ◯ 19−8

8 ◯ 12   12−7 ◯ 6   11 ◯ 6+6   12+5 ◯ 14+5

18 ◯ 16   13−8 ◯ 5   20 ◯ 5+15   18−8 ◯ 16−5

 Challenge and extension question

5 Fill in the ◯ with ">" or "<".

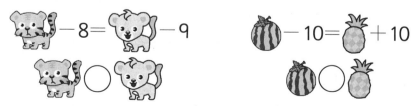

5.9   Mathematics playground (2)

 Learning objective

Add and subtract numbers to 20

 Basic questions

1 Work out these mentally. Write the answers.

$9 + 9 =$ $5 + 5 =$ $6 + 14 =$ $8 + 4 + 6 =$

$16 - 7 =$ $9 - 6 =$ $17 - 10 =$ $7 + 9 - 5 =$

$16 - 8 =$ $8 + 7 =$ $11 - 6 =$ $18 - 10 - 8 =$

2 Fill in the ☐ with the correct numbers.

$5 + \boxed{} = 11$ $12 - \boxed{} = 8$ $8 + 2 + \boxed{} = 16$

$\boxed{} + 10 = 19$ $16 - \boxed{} = 5$ $20 - 7 - \boxed{} = 0$

$12 + \boxed{} = 20$ $\boxed{} - 10 = 7$ $6 + \boxed{} - 8 = 2$

3 Use the three numbers given in each group to make two addition sentences and two subtraction sentences.

    4   8   12   3   13   10   8   8   0

    _____   _____   _____

    _____   _____   _____

    _____   _____   _____

    _____   _____   _____

4 Fill in the table.

Double it									Halve it
		10		4		3		8	
	12		18		10		14		

5 Put the towers in order from the tallest as the first.

(　) (　) (　) (　) (　) (　)

6 Look at the shape of each object. Then write the number of each object in the correct oval.

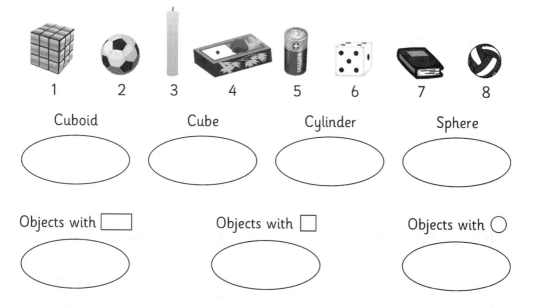

1　　2　　3　　4　　5　　6　　7　　8

Cuboid　　　　Cube　　　　Cylinder　　　　Sphere

◯　　　　◯　　　　◯　　　　◯

Objects with ▭　　　Objects with ☐　　　Objects with ◯

◯　　　　　◯　　　　　◯

 Challenge and extension question

7 Continue drawing 11 more beads following the pattern.

5.10　Mathematics playground (3)

 Learning objective

Use number bonds to add and subtract numbers to 20

 Basic questions

1 Work out these mentally. Write the answers.

$7+7=$　　$9+6=$　　$5+13=$　　$7+5+5=$

$12-7=$　　$18-6=$　　$18-10=$　　$4+8-5=$

$16-9=$　　$9+7=$　　$12-6=$　　$16-1-8=$

2 Fill in the boxes to complete the number line.

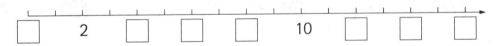

□　2　□　□　□　10　□　□　□

3 Put the eight numbers 5, 12, 0, 20, 8, 14, 10 and 3 in order starting from the least. _____

4 Fill in the numbers on each floor of the houses.

12	20	8	5
12+0	10+10	18–10	10–5
11+1	11+9	17–9	11–6
+	+	–	–
+	+	–	–
+	+	–	–

5 Fill in the number walls.

(a)
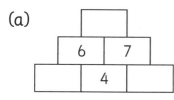

(b)
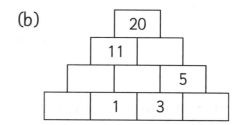

6 Fill in the ◯ with ">", "<" or "=" and the ☐ with numbers.

$5+9 \bigcirc 15$ $\qquad$ $12-4 \bigcirc 7$ $\qquad$ $4+6 \bigcirc 7+3$

$16-5 \bigcirc 11-5$ $\quad 9>2+\square$ $\qquad$ $\square+7<15$

$7>\square+4$ $\qquad$ $\square-5=7+\square$ $\quad 10-\square=\square-6$

Challenge and extension question

7 Fill in the ◯ using the numbers 4, 5, 6, 7, 8, 9, 10, 11 and 12 so that the sums of the 3 numbers on both lines are the same.

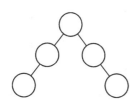
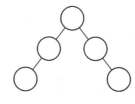
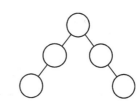

Unit test 5

1 Work out these mentally. Write the answers.

$9+4=$ $15-6=$ $5+7=$ $14-8=$ $16-7+5=$

$7+4=$ $17-9=$ $15-7=$ $10+8=$ $15-9-6=$

$14-8=$ $15-8=$ $9+7=$ $14-9=$ $12+8-5=$

$7+8=$ $9+3=$ $13-4=$ $6+7=$ $9+8+3=$

2 Look at the pictures and then write the number sentences.

By type			By size		
( )+( )=( )			( )+( )=( )		
( )+( )=( )			( )+( )=( )		
( )−( )=( )			( )−( )=( )		
( )−( )=( )			( )−( )=( )		

 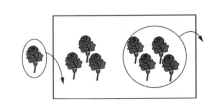

There are 16  in total.

How many  are in the basket?

□○□=□   □○□○□=□

❸ Fill in the brackets with numbers.

(a) 1 ten and 5 ones make (   ).

(b) There are (   ) ten and (   ) ones in 17.

(c) The sum of the greatest one-digit number and the least two-digit number is (   ).

(d) Put the numbers 18, 4, 15, 2, 20 and 0 in order starting from the greatest. (   )

4 Complete the number patterns.

11	12		15		

	7		3

10		6		2

		14		

❺ Fill in the blanks.

$6 \xrightarrow{\text{double}}$ _____

$8 \xrightarrow{\text{half}}$ _____ $\xrightarrow{\text{half}}$ _____

$20 \xrightarrow{\text{half}}$ _____ $\xrightarrow{\text{half}}$ _____

$7 \xrightarrow{\text{double}}$ _____

6 Work out these, then write your own calculations.

$3 + 11 =$

$20 - 3 =$

$17 - 8 =$

$4 + 10 =$

$18 - 5 =$

$15 - 8 =$

$5 + \underline{\quad} =$

$16 - \underline{\quad} =$

$13 - \underline{\quad} =$

$\underline{\quad} + \underline{\quad} =$

$\underline{\quad} - \underline{\quad} =$

$\underline{\quad} - \underline{\quad} =$

7 Fill in the number walls.

(a)

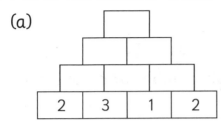

(b)

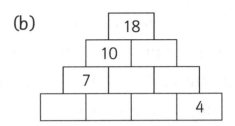

8 Fill in the $\bigcirc$ with ">", "<" or "=" and the $\square$ with the numbers.

$7+8 \bigcirc 15$ $12-3 \bigcirc 8$ $7+6 \bigcirc 8+5$

$16-5 \bigcirc 15-6$ $9>4+\square$ $20-\square<5$

$\square+6<12$ $17>\square+10$ $\square+7=\square-5$

$12-\square=\square-9$ $14-\square=7+\square$

9 Complete addition and subtraction tables.

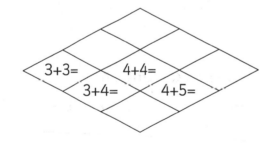

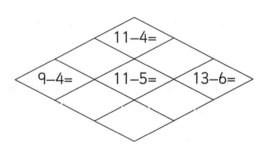

10 Write the number sentences and calculate.

(a) John has 8 storybooks and 5 science books. How many books does John have in total?

Number sentence: _____

(b) John had 15 books. He gave away 7 books. How many books did he still have?

Number sentence: _____

(c) 14 pupils in Class A have won an award. 9 of them are boys. How many are girls?

Number sentence: _____

(d) There were 7 ducks on the river. After a while, some ducks joined in. Now there are 12 ducks altogether. How many ducks joined in?

Number sentence: _____

(e) After 8 cars drove away from the car park, there were 12 cars left. How many cars were there at first?

Number sentence: _____

(f) There were 15 birds in the tree at first. 9 birds flew away. Then another 10 birds flew in to the tree. How many birds are in the tree now?

Number sentence: _____

11 Circle the one that does not belong to the group.

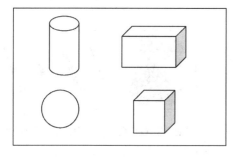 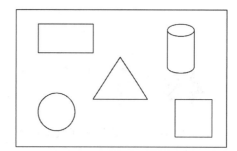

Chapter 6   Numbers up to 100

6.1   Tens and ones

 Learning objective

Partition numbers to 100 into tens and ones

 Basic questions

1 Count and then fill in the blanks.

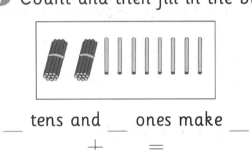

___ tens and ___ ones make ___

___ + ___ = ___

       ___ tens and ___ ones make ___

          ___ + ___ = ___

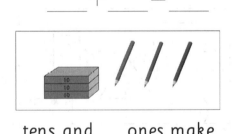

___ tens and ___ ones make ___

___ + ___ = ___

       ___ tens and ___ ones make ___

          ___ + ___ = ___

2 Group the objects into tens first, then count by tens and ones, record the result and finally write the numbers in numerals.

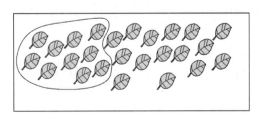

Tens	Ones

Written as: _____

Tens	Ones

Written as: _____

❸ Draw △ accordingly.

Tens	Ones
2	0

Tens	Ones
1	8

4 Fill in the ☐ with numbers.

(a) 50 is ☐ tens. 　3 tens are ☐. 　80 is ☐ tens.

　4 tens are ☐. 　100 is ☐ tens. 　☐ ones are 100.

(b) 26 = 20 + ☐ 　53 = ☐ + 3 　84 = 80 + ☐

　69 = ☐ + 9 　71 = 70 + ☐ 　45 = ☐ + ☐

Challenge and extension question

❺ Fill in the brackets.

(a) 5 tens and 2 ones make (　　). 4 ones and 9 tens make

　(　　).

(b) 63 is made up of (　　) tens and (　　) ones.

　There are (　　) tens and (　　) ones in 78.

(c) In the number 36, "3" is in the (　　) place. It means (　　)

　(　　). "6" is in the (　　) place. It means (　　 X 　　).

6.2 Knowing 100

 Learning objective

Add tens to tatal 100 and subtract tens from 100

 Basic questions

1 Complete the number lines.

```
|    |    |    |    |    |    |    |    |    |    |    →
0    10   20   □    □    □    60   □    □    □    □
```

```
|    |    |    |    |    |    |    |    |    |    |    →
0    10   □    30   □    50   □    70   □    90   □
```

2 Fill numbers in the blanks using the 100 square diagram below.

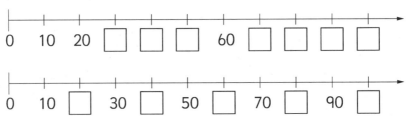

3 tens are _____.

5 tens are _____

8 tens are _____

There are _____ groups of 10 in 100.

There are _____ groups of 50 in 100.

There are _____ groups of 25 in 100.

3 Calculate using the 100 square diagram in Question 2.

$10 + 40 =$	$100 - 60 =$	$90 - 50 =$
$20 + 40 =$	$90 - 50 =$	$80 - 50 =$
$30 + 40 =$	$80 - 40 =$	$70 - 50 =$
$40 + 40 =$	$70 - 30 =$	$60 - 50 =$
$50 + 40 =$	$60 - 20 =$	$50 - 50 =$

$10 + 90 =$	$90 + \underline{\quad} = 100$	$100 - \underline{\quad} = 50$
$20 + 70 =$	$80 + \underline{\quad} = 100$	$100 - \underline{\quad} = 40$
$30 + 50 =$	$70 + \underline{\quad} = 100$	$100 - \underline{\quad} = 30$
$40 + 30 =$	$60 + \underline{\quad} = 100$	$100 - \underline{\quad} = 20$
$50 + 10 =$	$50 + \underline{\quad} = 100$	$100 - \underline{\quad} = 10$

4 Calculate using the diagrams.

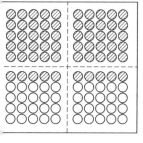 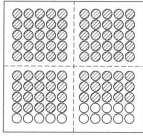 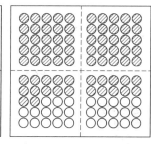 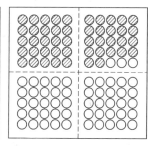

$50 + (\quad) = 100 \qquad 85 + (\quad) = 100 \qquad 72 + (\quad) = 100 \qquad 47 + (\quad) = 100$

Challenge and extension question

5 Use a pattern to complete the number sentences.

(a)

$10 + (\quad) = 100$	$92 + (\quad) = 100$
$15 + (\quad) = 100$	$82 + (\quad) = 100$
$20 + (\quad) = 100$	$72 + (\quad) = 100$
$25 + (\quad) = 100$	$62 + (\quad) = 100$

(b)

$100 - (\quad) = 11$	$100 - (\quad) = 99$
$100 - (\quad) = 21$	$100 - (\quad) = 89$
$100 - (\quad) = 31$	$100 - (\quad) = 79$
$100 - (\quad) = 41$	$100 - (\quad) = 69$

6.3 Representing numbers up to 100 (1)

 Learning objective

Recognise the place value of 2-digit numbers

 Basic questions

1 Count the dots and then write the numbers.

(a)

Tens	Ones
•• ••	••• •••

Tens place	Ones place

Written as: _____

(b)

Tens	Ones
••• ••	• •

Tens place	Ones place

Written as: _____

(c)

Tens	Ones
•••• ••••	

Tens place	Ones place

Written as: _____

2 Fill in the blanks and draw the dots. The first one has been done for you.

(a)

Tens place	Ones place
3	5

Written as: 3 5

Tens	Ones
• • •	•• •• •

(b)

Tens place	Ones place

Written as: 6 8

Tens	Ones

(c)

Tens place	Ones place

Written as:
5 4

Tens	Ones

(d)

Tens place	Ones place

Written as:
7 0

Tens	Ones

❸ Draw a line to match.

(a)
| Ones place: 2 |
| Tens place: 7 |

(b) | 5 tens and 9 ones |

(c) | 3   8 |

| 2   7 |

| 7   2 |

| 5   9 |

| 9   5 |

| 8 tens and 3 ones |

| 3 tens and 8 ones |

Challenge and extension question

❹ Fill in the brackets.

(a) 9 tens and 5 ones make (   ). 6 tens and 1 one make (   ).

(b) 47 is made up of (   ) tens and (   ) ones.

   52 is made up of (   ) tens and (   ).

(c) In a number 84, "4" is in the (   ) place. It means (   )
   (   ). "8" is in the (   ) place. It means (   ) (   ).

6.4 Representing numbers up to 100 (2)

 Learning objective

Recognise and compare numbers to 100

 Basic questions

1 Answer the questions using the number lines.

(a) Mark 8, 26, 41, 57, 74, 88 and 92 on the number line.

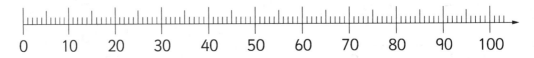

(b) Write the numbers that a, b, c, d, e, f, g and h represent.

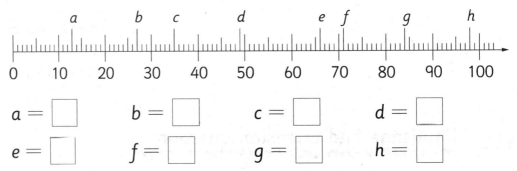

a = ☐   b = ☐   c = ☐   d = ☐

e = ☐   f = ☐   g = ☐   h = ☐

(c) Write the numbers before and after a, b, c, d, e, f, g and h.

	a				b				c				d	
	e				f				g				h	

(d) Write the tens numbers before and after a, b, c, d, e, f, g and h.

	a				b				c				d	
	e				f				g				h	

2 Write the following numbers in the circles.

72	90	49	78	15	93	70	100
65	81	5	27	77	35	79	95

7 in the tens place   5 in the ones place   Greater than 80

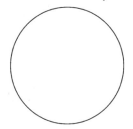 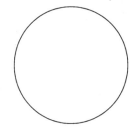 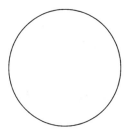

3 Write all the two-digit numbers based on the information given.

(a) The digit in the ones place is 3: _____

(b) The digit in the tens place is 6: _____

(c) The digit in the tens place is 5: _____

(d) It is greater than 48 and has the same digit in the tens place and ones place: _____

(e) It has 7 in its tens place and the digit in its ones place is 7 less than the digit in the tens place: _____.

 Challenge and extension question

4 Write the two-digit numbers.

The digit in the ones place is 2 greater than that in the tens place. Write all such two-digit numbers. _____

The digit in the tens place is 2 greater than that in the ones place. Write all such numbers. _____

6.5 Comparing numbers within 100 (1)

 Learning objective

Compare and order numbers to 100

 Basic questions

1 Mark 18, 23, 32, 55, 68, 71 and 97 on the number line.

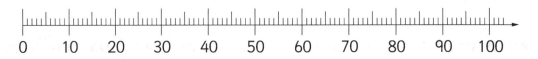

2 Write the numbers indicated.

(a) Write the numbers that a, b, c, d, e, f, g and h represent.

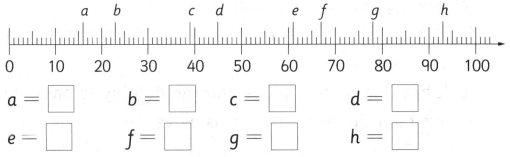

a = ☐   b = ☐   c = ☐   d = ☐

e = ☐   f = ☐   g = ☐   h = ☐

(b) Write the tens numbers that are before and after a, b, c, d, e, f, g and h.

	a			b			c			d	

	e			f			g			h	

3 Find patterns and fill in with suitable numbers.

26		28		30			33	58		62			

	85			79	77					71			

4 Fill in the ◯ with ">", "<" or "=".

20 ◯ 30   13 ◯ 31   29 ◯ 30   100 ◯ 90

45 ◯ 55   27 ◯ 21   69 ◯ 50   54 ◯ 45

62 ◯ 58   0 ◯ 100   70 ◯ 71   66 ◯ 63

89 ◯ 90   46 ◯ 64   39 ◯ 40   100 ◯ 50 + 50

5 Put the numbers in order from the least to the greatest.

(a) 27   19   91   74   58   93

(   )<(   )<(   )<(   )<(   )<(   )

(b) 6   46   76   86   60   96

(   )<(   )<(   )<(   )<(   )<(   )

6 Write the following numbers into the (   ) as indicated.

90   15   28   39   47   56   34   71

The numbers greater than 45 are (   ).

The numbers less than 45 are (   ).

Challenge and extension question

7 It is a two-digit number. The difference between the digits in the ones place and the tens place is 3. Write all the two-digit numbers that answer the clue.

6.6 Comparing numbers within 100 (2)

 Learning objective

Position, compare and order numbers to 100

Basic questions

1 Fill in the boxes.

4 tens make ☐.   6 tens make ☐.   2 tens make ☐.

There are ☐ tens and ☐ ones in 56.

There are ☐ tens and ☐ ones in 82.

☐ tens and ☐ ones make 36.

☐ tens and ☐ ones make 98.

2 (a) Write the number that comes before each number.

___ 30   ___ 67   ___ 79   ___ 90   ___ 51

(b) Write the number that comes after each number.

40 ___   59 ___   67 ___   84 ___   99 ___

(c) Write the numbers that come before and after each number.

___ 63 ___   ___ 50 ___   ___ 61 ___   ___ 48 ___

(d) Write the tens numbers that come before and after each number.

___ 26 ___   ___ 58 ___   ___ 77 ___   ___ 80 ___

3 Fill in the ( ) and mark the numbers on the number line.

(a) The number that comes before 84 is ( ). The third number after 84 is ( ).

```
|‧‧|‧‧|‧‧|‧‧|‧‧|‧‧|‧‧|‧‧|‧‧|‧‧|‧‧|‧‧|‧‧|‧‧|‧‧|‧‧|‧‧|‧‧|‧‧|‧‧|→
0    10   20   30   40   50   60   70   80   90   100
```

(b) The fourth number that comes after 68 is _____ . The tens number that comes before 94 is _____ .

```
|‧‧|‧‧|‧‧|‧‧|‧‧|‧‧|‧‧|‧‧|‧‧|‧‧|‧‧|‧‧|‧‧|‧‧|‧‧|‧‧|‧‧|‧‧|‧‧|‧‧|→
0    10   20   30   40   50   60   70   80   90   100
```

4 Fill in the ◯ with ">", "<" or "=".

47 ◯ 74   100 ◯ 10   48 ◯ 4 tens and 8 ones

33 ◯ 31   64 ◯ 34   86 ◯ 8 ones and 6 tens

72 ◯ 76   89 ◯ 98   10 ◯ 10 ones

17 ◯ 77   30 ◯ 60   64 ◯ 46 ones

5 Put the numbers in order from the greatest to the least.

(a) 66   86   17   99   27   88

( )>( )>( )>( )>( )>( )

(b) 100   26   44   39   71   65

( )>( )>( )>( )>( )>( )

Challenge and extension question

6 Write suitable numbers from 18, 80, 8, 78, 38, 82, 89, 88, 58 and 28 in the boxes below.

in the ones place	8 in the tens place	Greater than 50	Less than 50

6.7 Practice and exercise (I)

 Learning objective

Compare and partition 2-digit numbers

Basic questions

① Mark 38, 42, 59, 81, 9, 76 and 95 on the number line.

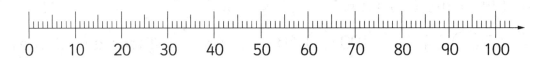

② Fill in the ◯ with ">", "<" or "=".

39 ◯ 30   41 ◯ 31   73 ◯ 49   51 ◯ 89

80 ◯ 79   6 ◯ 66   65 ◯ 38   10 ◯ 24

③ Find the nearest numbers by adding 1 or subtracting 1.

$16 - 1 =$	$29 - 1 =$	$87 - 1 =$
$16 + 1 =$	$29 + 1 =$	$87 + 1 =$
$60 - 1 =$	$99 - 1 =$	$50 - 1 =$
$60 + 1 =$	$99 + 1 =$	$50 + 1 =$

④ Write the numbers that come before and after each number.

____ 27 ____   ____ 49 ____   ____ 65 ____   ____ 43 ____

____ 81 ____   ____ 30 ____   ____ 77 ____   ____ 62 ____

⑤ Write the tens numbers that come before and after each number.

___ 39 ___   ___ 78 ___   ___ 51 ___   ___ 62 ___

___ 40 ___   ___ 80 ___   ___ 65 ___   ___ 98 ___

⑥ Get back to the tens.

$31 - \underline{\hspace{1cm}} = 30$	$89 - \underline{\hspace{1cm}} = 80$	$26 - \underline{\hspace{1cm}} = 20$
$32 - \underline{\hspace{1cm}} = 30$	$77 - \underline{\hspace{1cm}} = 70$	$49 - \underline{\hspace{1cm}} = 40$
$33 - \underline{\hspace{1cm}} = 30$	$65 - \underline{\hspace{1cm}} = 60$	$64 - \underline{\hspace{1cm}} = 60$
$34 - \underline{\hspace{1cm}} = 30$	$53 - \underline{\hspace{1cm}} = 50$	$87 - \underline{\hspace{1cm}} = 80$

⑦ Add up to the tens.

$1 + \underline{\hspace{1cm}} = 10$	$19 + \underline{\hspace{1cm}} = 20$	$22 + \underline{\hspace{1cm}} = 30$
$31 + \underline{\hspace{1cm}} = 40$	$28 + \underline{\hspace{1cm}} = 30$	$57 + \underline{\hspace{1cm}} = 60$
$51 + \underline{\hspace{1cm}} = 60$	$37 + \underline{\hspace{1cm}} = 40$	$63 + \underline{\hspace{1cm}} = 70$
$71 + \underline{\hspace{1cm}} = 80$	$46 + \underline{\hspace{1cm}} = 50$	$76 + \underline{\hspace{1cm}} = 80$

⑧ Calculate with reasoning.

$16 + 4 =$	$18 + 2 =$	$7 + 23 =$
$26 + 4 =$	$38 + 2 =$	$7 + 43 =$
$36 + 4 =$	$58 + 2 =$	$7 + 63 =$
$46 + 4 =$	$78 + 2 =$	$7 + 83 =$

 Challenge and extension question

⑨ Make up to the tens.

$58 + (\quad) = (\quad)$ $65 - (\quad) = (\quad)$

$74 + (\quad) = (\quad)$ $87 - (\quad) = (\quad)$

$(\quad) + 41 = (\quad)$ $(\quad) - 4 = (\quad)$

$(\quad) + 62 = (\quad)$ $(\quad) - 9 = (\quad)$

6.8 Knowing money (1)

 Learning objective

Recognise, describe and compare quantities of money

 Basic questions

1. Write the value of coins.

(   ) penny   (   ) pence   (   ) pence   (   ) pound

(   ) pence   (   ) pence   (   ) pence   (   ) pounds

2. Put the values of the coins in Question 1 in order, starting from the greatest.

_____

3. Write the values of the notes.

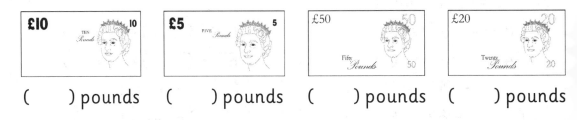

(   ) pounds   (   ) pounds   (   ) pounds   (   ) pounds

Put the values of the notes in order, starting from the least.

_____

4 Fill in the blanks. The first one has been done for you.

(a) One ⬢ = Two ⬢   (b) One ⬢ = _____ ⬢

(c) One ⬢ = _____ ⬢   (d) One ⬢ = _____ ⬢

(e) One ⬢ = _____ ⬢   (f) One ⬢ = _____ ⬢

5 Joan paid exactly 10 pounds for a maths book.

(a) If she used only one note to pay, the value of the note is _____ .

(b) If she used two notes to pay, the value of each note is _____ .

(c) If she used one note and three coins to pay, the values of the note and the coins are _____ .

Challenge and extension question

6 How can you make up 18 pence using four coins? How about five coins? Use number sentences to show all the possible ways. (Hint: You can use the same coin more than once.)

Four coins: _____

Five coins: _____

6.9 Knowing money (2)

 Learning objective

Recognise, describe and compare quantities of money

 Basic questions

1 Look at the pictures and fill the amount of money in the brackets.

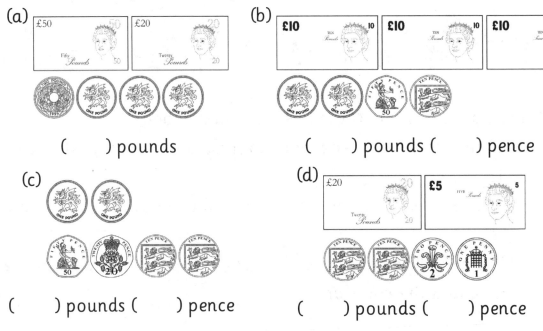

(a) (　　　) pounds

(b) (　　　) pounds (　　　) pence

(c) (　　　) pounds (　　　) pence

(d) (　　　) pounds (　　　) pence

2 Fill in the brackets.

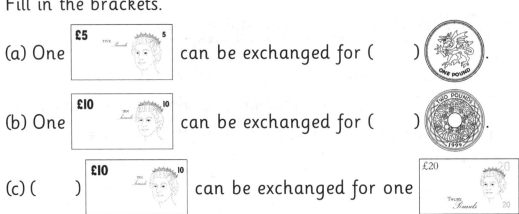

(a) One £5 can be exchanged for (　　　).

(b) One £10 can be exchanged for (　　　).

(c) (　　　) £10 can be exchanged for one £20.

③ Fill in the ◯ with ">", "<" or "=".

80p ◯ 50p   £15 ◯ £20   £30 ◯ 30 pence

6 pounds ◯ 60 pence   28p ◯ 3 pounds   42p ◯ £4 and 2p

④ Write the number sentences to show how to make up £20 as indicated below.

Using three notes: _____

Using three notes and three coins: _____

Challenge and extension question

⑤ Write the number sentences to solve word problems.

£18   £8   £15   £5

(a) Joan bought a pencil box. She gave the cashier £20. How much change should she get?

Number sentence: _____

(b) Amy bought one book and one pencil sharpener. How much did she spend in total?

Number sentence: _____

(c) Martin bought a pair of scissors and got £2 change. How much did he give the cashier?

Number sentence: _____

Unit test 6

1 Count and then fill in the blanks.

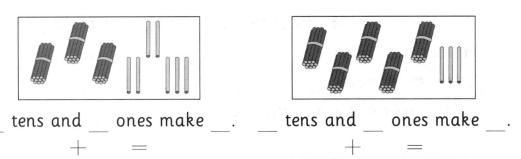

___ tens and ___ ones make ___ .   ___ tens and ___ ones make ___ .

___ + ___ = ___   ___ + ___ = ___

2 Fill in the blanks.

(a) In the number 82, "8" is in the _____ place. It means _____

_____ . "2" is in the _____ place. It means _____ _____ .

(b) 5 ones make _____ . 5 tens make _____ .

(c) 4 tens and 7 ones make _____ .

(d) _____ ones and _____ tens make 38.

(e) A two-digit number has 9 in the tens place and 2 in the ones

place. This two-digit number is _____ .

3 Answer the questions based on the number line.

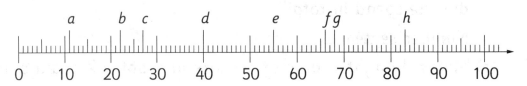

(a) Write the numbers that a, b, c, d, e, f, g and h represent.

$a = \boxed{}$ $b = \boxed{}$ $c = \boxed{}$ $d = \boxed{}$

$e = \boxed{}$ $f = \boxed{}$ $g = \boxed{}$ $h = \boxed{}$

(b) Write the numbers that come before and after a, b and c.

	a				b				c	

(c) Write the tens numbers that come before and after d, e and f.

	d				e				f	

4 Fill in the (   ) with suitable numbers.

(a) £50 £50   (b) £50 £10   (c) £10

(   ) pounds   (   ) pounds

(   ) pounds
(   ) pence

5 Exchange the same amount of money.

(a) One £50 can be exchanged for (   ) £10 .

(b) One £20 can be exchanged for (   ) £10 .

(c) One £10 can be exchanged for (   ) .

(d) One £5 can be exchanged for (   ) FIVE PENCE .

6 Solving word problems.

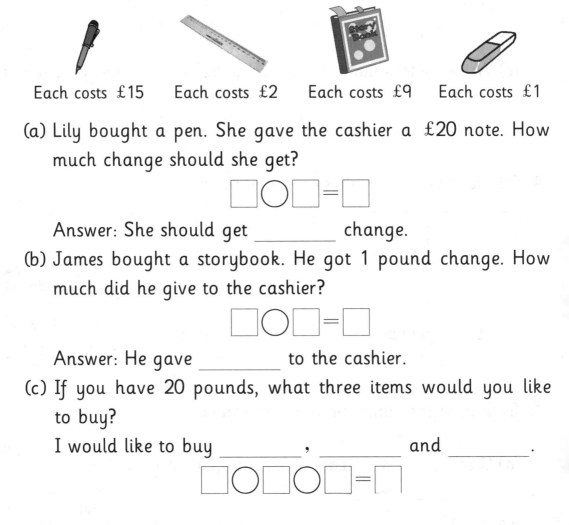

Each costs £15   Each costs £2   Each costs £9   Each costs £1

(a) Lily bought a pen. She gave the cashier a £20 note. How much change should she get?

☐ ◯ ☐ = ☐

Answer: She should get _____ change.

(b) James bought a storybook. He got 1 pound change. How much did he give to the cashier?

☐ ◯ ☐ = ☐

Answer: He gave _____ to the cashier.

(c) If you have 20 pounds, what three items would you like to buy?

I would like to buy _____ , _____ and _____ .

☐ ◯ ☐ ◯ ☐ = ☐

Chapter 7   Introduction to time (I)

7.1   Year, month and day

Learning objective

Recognise and use language relating to days, weeks, months and years

Basic questions

1. Fill in the brackets.

   (a) There are (   ) months in a year. They are January, February, March, (   ), May, June, (   ), August, September, (   ), November and (   ).
   This month is (   ).

   (b) There are (   ) days in a week. They are Sunday, (   ), Tuesday, Wednesday, (   ), Friday and (   ). Today is (   ).

2. Put the following in order starting from winter.

   | Spring | Autumn | Winter | Summer |

   _____

3. An event starts on 16 May 2016, Monday and lasts 4 days.

   (a) Which date is the last day of the event? Write the date in words and numbers and in numbers only.
   In words and numbers: _____ and in

numbers only: _____

(b) Did the event take place on Friday of the same week?

Answer: _____ (Write yes or no.)

4 Complete the table to show public holidays in 2016.

	Dates in words and numbers	Dates in numbers	Day of the week
New Year's Day	1 January 2016		Friday
Good Friday		25/03/2016	
Christmas Day	25 December 2016		Sunday
Boxing Day		26/12/2016	

Challenge and extension question

5 On which day did your school's recent Easter holidays start, and on which day did they end?

(a) Write the dates in words and numbers and in numbers only.

Start Date:

In words and numbers: _____. In numbers

_____

End Date:

In words and numbers: _____. In numbers

_____

(b) What days of the week did they fall on?

Start Date: _____

End Date: _____

(c) How many days did the Easter Holidays last?

Answer: _____ days

7.2   Telling the time

Learning objective

Read the time to the hour and half past the hour

Basic questions

1 Put the following times in order starting from the earliest.

(a) tomorrow, yesterday, today

_____

(b) evening, afternoon, morning, noon

_____

2 What can you complete in a minute and in an hour? Put a tick (√) for each activity. The first one has been done for you.

	In a minute	In an hour
(a) Writing ten words	(√)	( )
(b) Reading a story book	( )	( )
(c) Drinking a cup of water	( )	( )
(d) Attending a dancing class	( )	( )
(e) Putting pencils into a pencil case	( )	( )

3 Fill in the brackets with suitable units of time (minute or hour).

(a) Amy spends 8 ( ) at school per school day.

(b) John lives close to the school. It takes him only 10 ( ) to walk to the school.

(c) Tom's music lesson lasted one ( ).

(d) Jenny took 30 ( ) to finish her lunch.

4 Draw a line to match the time. One has been done for you.

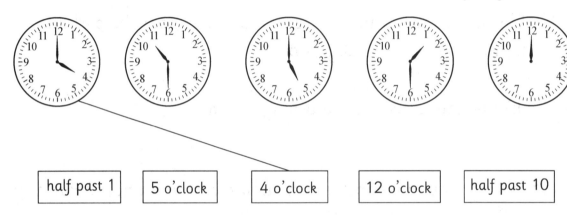

| half past 1 | 5 o'clock | 4 o'clock | 12 o'clock | half past 10 |

5 Where is the minute hand? Draw to show your answer.

2:00   9:00   6:00

 Challenge and extension question

6 Write four activities you did today (for example, having breakfast), and put them in order starting from the earliest.

7.3   Hour and half an hour

1️⃣ Read the following clocks. Circle the box that shows the right time.

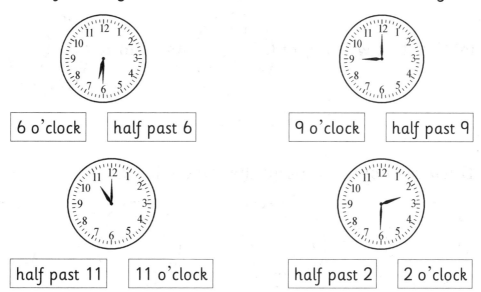

| 6 o'clock | half past 6 |

| 9 o'clock | half past 9 |

| half past 11 | 11 o'clock |

| half past 2 | 2 o'clock |

2️⃣ Draw a line to match.

| 10:00 | 07:30 | 06:00 | 03:30 |

3️⃣ Put the times in order starting from the earliest.

| 3 o'clock afternoon | half past 5 | half past 9 evening |
| 1 o'clock afternoon | 12 noon | 5 o'clock afternoon |

4 Read the time and then fill in the blanks.

(a) The exam starts at  . It ends at

_____   _____

(b) We start walking at  and end at .

_____   _____

5 Draw the hour hand and the minute hand.

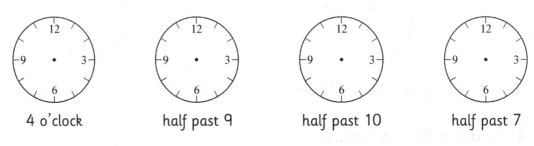

4 o'clock   half past 9   half past 10   half past 7

 Challenge and extension question

6 Which of the following clocks does not work properly? Put a
"✕" to indicate your answer.

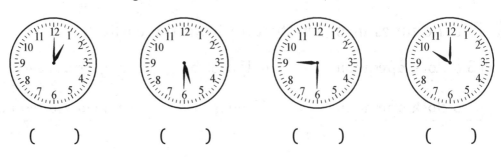

(   )   (   )   (   )   (   )

Unit test 7

1 Put the following months in order starting from the earliest of a year: September, June, January, December, August, April

_____

2 If today is Monday, then yesterday was (   ), the day before yesterday was (   ), tomorrow will be (   ) and the day after tomorrow will be (   ).

3 Draw a line to match.

| 06:30 | 08:00 | 10:30 | 02:00 |

4 Write the times in order, starting from the earliest.

| 3 o'clock afternoon | 8 o'clock morning | half past 11 |
| half past 9 evening | 4 o'clock afternoon | 12 noon |

_____

_____

⑤ Complete the table to show the public holidays in 2017.

	Dates in words and numbers	Dates in numbers	Day of the week
New Year's Day			Sunday
Good Friday	14 April 2017		
Spring Bank Holiday		29/05/2017	Monday
Christmas Day			Monday
Boxing Day	26 December 2017		

⑥ Write suitable units of time (minute, hour or day).

(a) A lesson lasts 35 _____.

(b) A movie lasts 2 _____.

(c) Ben walks from home to school in 15 _____.

(d) There are 14 _____ in two weeks.

(e) On Saturday, Joan and her parents spent 5 _____ visiting a theme park.

⑦ Draw the hour hand and minute hand on each clock face to show the given time.

7 o'clock

5 o'clock

half past 4

half past 9

8 Look at the clocks and fill in the blanks accordingly.

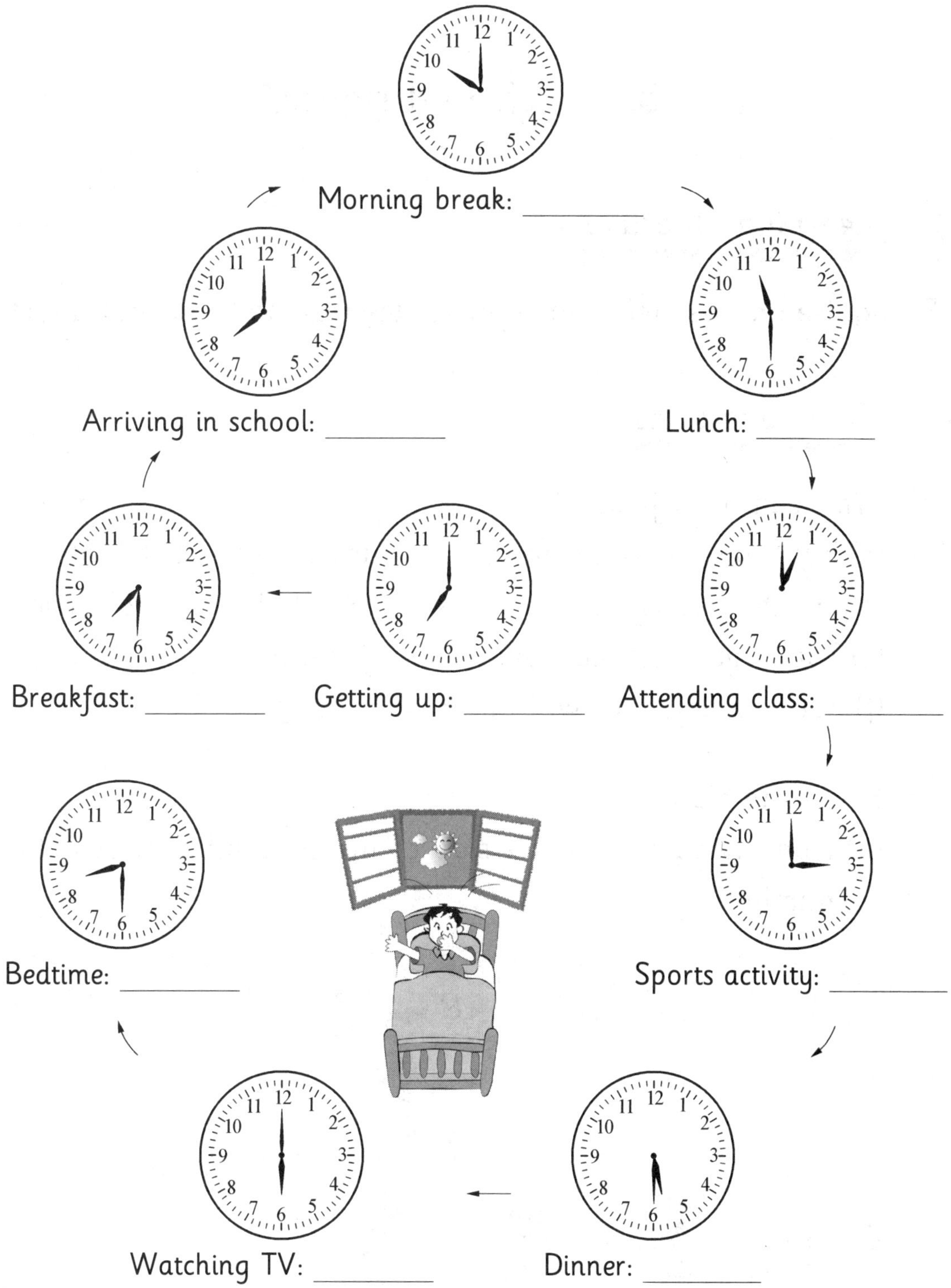

Morning break: _____

Arriving in school: _____

Lunch: _____

Breakfast: _____

Getting up: _____

Attending class: _____

Bedtime: _____

Sports activity: _____

Watching TV: _____

Dinner: _____

Chapter 8   Let's practise geometry

8.1   Left and right (1)

 Learning objective

Recognise and use left and right to describe position and direction

 Basic questions

1 Who can do it fast?
   (a) Put out your right hand.   (b) Lift your left foot.
   (c) Touch your left ear.   (d) Blink your right eye.
   (e) Touch your left ear with your left hand.
   (f) Pat your left foot with your right hand.

2 Fill in the blanks.
   (a) I am living on the left side of house number 8. It is house
       number _____.

(b)

   (i) is on the _____ side of and on the _____ side of

(ii) 🐰 is on the ＿＿ side of 🐸 and on the ＿＿ side of 🐱.

(c) (i) The children coming downstairs are on the ＿＿＿＿＿
side and those going upstairs are on the ＿＿＿＿＿
side.

(ii) We walk on the ＿＿＿＿＿ hand side of the
road so we can see oncoming traffic.

(d)

(i) Counting from the left, the banana is in the (   ) place.
On its left is (   ).

(ii) There are (   ) fruits on the left of the pear. The grapes
are on its (   ).

(iii) There are (   ) types of fruits altogether. The first fruit
from the left is (   ).

Challenge and extension question

❸ Fill in the (   ) with letters to stand for the animals.

A   B   C   D   E   F

(a) On the left of the zebra are (   ), and on its right are (   ).

(b) The kangaroo is on the (   ) of the zebra. The duck is on
the (   ) of the rabbit.

(c) There are (   ) animals on the right of the rabbit and there
are (   ) animals on its left.

(d) (   ) is the sixth from the right and the sheep is the (   )
from the left.

8.2 Left and right (2)

Recognise and use left and right to describe position and direction

 Basic questions

1 Read the instructions below and then draw a line to put each flower in its correct place on the shelves.

(a) On the left of the daffodils is a tulip. The daisy is on its right.

(b) On the left of the plum flower is orchid.

(c) On the right of the rose is the sunflower.

2 Look at the grid and answer the questions below.

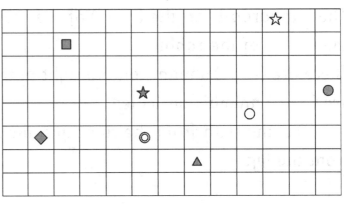

(a) Starting from ▲, move 3 squares up and draw a □. Again starting from ▲, move 5 squares left and draw a ◇.

(b) Starting from ★, move 5 squares right and 3 squares down, and then draw a △.

(c) Moving ○ 1 square down and _____ squares left will reach ◎.

❸ Looking for food.

(a) To reach the 🍎, 〰 needs to move ( ) squares left and ( ) square down.

(b) To get the 🥕, 🐰 needs to move ( ) square to the ( ) and then ( ) squares up.

(c) Use "→" to show how 🐰 should go to get 🥕.

Challenge and extension question

④ Draw a line to match.

Can you help the animals find their homes?

1 2 3 4

On the right of my home is Kitty's.

Kitty lives on the left of my home

On the left of frog's home is mine.

I am Kitty. Where is my home?

8.3   Left, centre and right, top, middle and bottom

 Learning objective

Solve position and movement problems on grids

 Basic questions

1 Guess who lives on each floor.
Joan, John and Tom decorated
their balconies with flowers.
Joan's flat is below John's.
John's flat is below Tom's.

Joan lives on the _____ floor.
John lives on the _____ floor.
Tom lives on the _____ floor.

2 Look at the picture.

Who is living:
(a) on the middle floor? _____
(b) on the top floor? _____
(c) on the bottom floor? _____
(d) next to the zebra's room? _____
(e) above the chick's room? _____
(f) just below the rabbit's room? _____

3 Fill in the grid with numbers.

(a) 10 is in the centre of the grid.

9 is above 10; 2 is on the right of 9.

1 is below 10; 8 is on the left of 1.

3 is on the left of 10; 4 is above 3.

5 is on the right of 10; 7 is below 5.

(b) 5 is in the centre of the grid.

2 is on the right of 8; 7 is below 5.

10 is on the left of 7; 8 is above 5.

3 is on the left of 5; 4 is above 3.

5 is on the left of 1; 6 is on the right of 7.

Challenge and extension question

4 Look at the grid and write directions or routes to the destinations. (■ means obstruction.)

(a) Starting from A

_____

_____

_____

Reach ☆

(b) Starting from B

_____

_____

_____

Reach △

(c) Starting from C

Move 1 grid right.

Move 3 grids up.

Move 5 grids left.

Reach _____

8.4   Comparing lengths

 Learning objective

Describe and compare lengths of objects

 Basic questions

1 Which shadow is longer? Put a "√" in the box.

☐   ☐

2 Compare the heights of the animals. Put a "○" against the tallest and a "△" against the shortest.

☐   ☐   ☐

3 Put a "△" against the shortest pencil and a "○" against the longest one in the (   ).

(   )

(   )

(   )

4 Put a "√" against the shortest and a "○" against the longest.

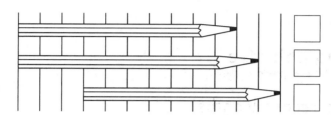

5 Put a "√" against the shortest rope and a "○" against the longest.

 Challenge and extension question

6 Which monkey has the longer way to reach banana? Put a "√" in the box.

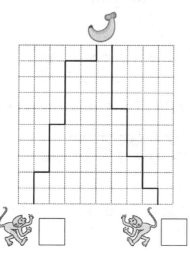

8.5 Length and height (1)

 Learning objective

Measure and record lengths

 Basic questions

1 Which measuring methods are correct? Put a " √ " accordingly.

length 4 cm
☐

length 10 cm
☐

length 5 cm
☐

length 6 cm
☐

2 Take a measure of the length.

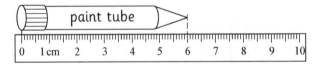

The length of the paint tube is (   ) cm.

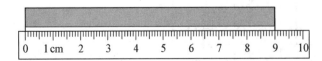

The length of the paper strip is (   ) cm.

The pencil is (   ) cm long.

3 Try it out yourself. Use a ruler to measure the following.

The width: The length: The length:

(   ) cm   (   ) cm   (   ) cm

Challenge and extension question

4 Fill in the (   ) with suitable units of length.

Height: Height: Length:

95 (   )   2 (   )   10 (   )

Height: Length: Height:

about 2(   )   about 60 (   )   about 4 (   )

8.6 Length and height (2)

 Learning objective

Measure and record lengths

Basic questions

1 Use a ruler to measure the lengths and fill in the brackets.
   (a) The rope is (   ) cm long. If it is cut by 4 cm, it will be
       (   ) cm long.

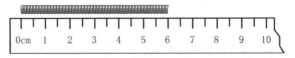

   (b) The snail has covered _____ cm. It has _____ cm to
       reach the end point.

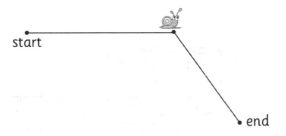

2 Fill in the (   ).

3 Fill in the (   ) with suitable units of length.
   James is 98 (   ) tall.
   The height of a door is 2 (   ).

The length of the shoe is 18 (   ).

The length of the rubber is 3 (   ).

The jumping rope is 3 (   ) long.

The length of the sports field is 100 (   ).

Challenge and extension question

4 Application problems.

(a) [image] is 90 cm tall. [image] is 98 cm tall. How many centimetres

taller is [image] than [image] ?

Answer: _____

(b) A rope is 80 metres long. It was cut by 8 metres for making

the [image]. How many metres are there left?

Answer: _____

8.7　Practice and exercise (II)

Describe and compare different quantities of length and time

 Basic questions

1

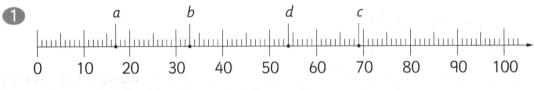

(a) Mark 27, 49, 85 and 92 on the number line.

(b) Write the numbers that come before and after a and b.

	a	

	b	

(c) Write the tens numbers that come before and after c and d.

	c	

	d	

2 Fill in the brackets.

5	3	0	9	2	6	8

(a) There are (　　) number cards altogether.

(b) Counting from the left, the second card is (　　) and the fifth card is (　　).

(c) 0 is the (　　) card if you count from the (　　).

(d) Arrange the cards above in order, starting from the greatest.

3 Measure the length and then fill in the brackets. Which way is shorter for the snail to visit the rabbit? Put a " √ " on one side of the shape to show your answer.

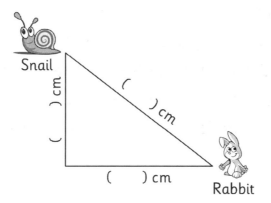

Snail

( ) cm

( ) cm

( ) cm

Rabbit

4 School trip to the zoo. Write the time in each box.

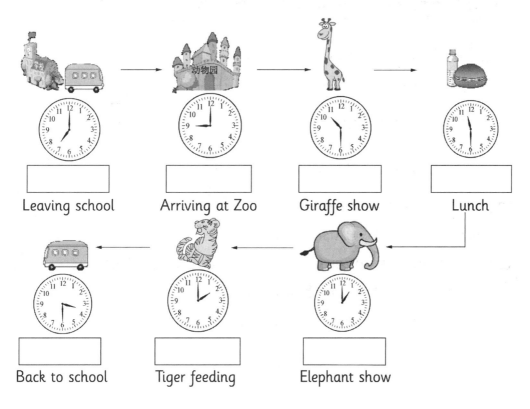

Leaving school   Arriving at Zoo   Giraffe show   Lunch

Back to school   Tiger feeding   Elephant show

5 Fill in the brackets.

(a) The digit in the tens place of 47 is (   ). It means (   )

(   ).

(b) 3 ones and 7 tens make (　　). It is (　　) greater than the least two-digit number.

(c) The tens nearest to 68 is (　　). The difference between these two numbers is (　　).

(d) A number has 6 in its tens place, and the digit in its ones place is 2 greater than that in the tens place. It is (　　).

(e) If you arrange the numbers 20, 42, 6, 89, 100 and 12 in order from the least to the greatest, the fourth number will be (　　).

Challenge and extension questions

6 Snail and ant are having a race.

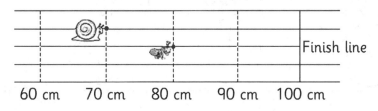

60 cm　　70 cm　　80 cm　　90 cm　　100 cm

(a) The ant has covered _____ cm and it is _____ cm away from the finish line.

(b) The snail has covered _____ cm and it has _____ cm left to reach the finish line.

(c) _____ will likely reach the finish line first.

Unit test 8

1 Use a ruler to measure each length and then fill in the brackets.

(a)

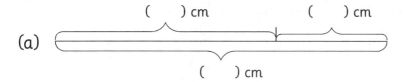

(   ) cm   (   ) cm

(   ) cm

(b) The little snail is going home.

I have moved _____ cm and still have _____ cm left.

2 Choose a suitable unit, and put a "√" in the ○ accordingly.

The height of the camel is about 2 m ○   cm ○

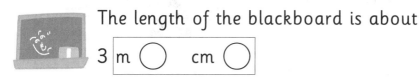

The length of the blackboard is about 3 m ○   cm ○

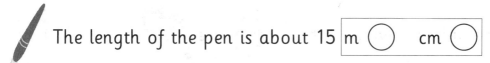

The length of the pen is about 15 m ○   cm ○

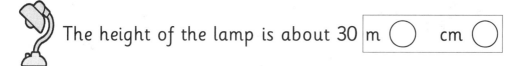

The height of the lamp is about 30 m ○   cm ○

3 Compare the lengths and then fill in the (   ).

(   ) is the longest. (   ) is the shortest.

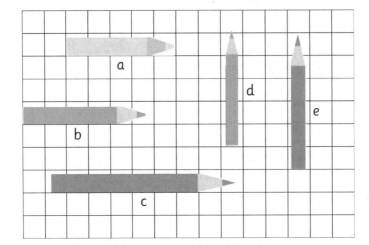

A. pencil a
B. pencil b
C. pencil c
D. pencil d
E. pencil e

4 In the picture showing ⬚, the animal living in the ■ is (   ).

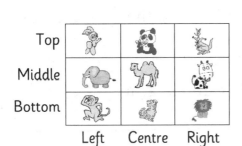

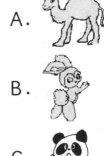

A.

B.

C.

5 The animals living next to are and (   ).

A.

B.

C.

End of year test

1 Work out these mentally. Write the answers. (10%)

$11 - 4 =$ $9 + 9 =$ $2 + 6 =$ $9 - 2 =$

$6 - 5 =$ $7 - 4 =$ $6 + 4 =$ $10 - 6 =$

$10 + 10 =$ $3 - 0 =$

2 Write the numbers that come before and after. (2%)

	39	

3 Find a pattern and then fill in with numbers. (2%)

	20	30		50	

4 Fill in the ◯ with ">", "<" or "=" and ☐ with numbers.
(16%)

$25 \bigcirc 28$ $75 \bigcirc 75 - 1$ $0 + 5 \bigcirc 10 - 5$

$\square > 96$ $10 - \square < 4$ $7 + \square > 11 - 3$

88 pence $\bigcirc$ 1 pound   50 pence $\bigcirc$ 5 pounds

5 Find patterns and then fill in the brackets with numbers (4%)

$8 + 8 = 16$ $20 - 10 = 10$

$9 + 7 = 16$ $20 - 8 = 12$

$10 + (\quad) = 16$ $20 - 6 = (\quad)$

$(\quad) + (\quad) = 16$ $20 - (\quad) = (\quad)$

6 Complete the addition table. (3%)

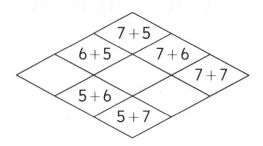

7 Fill in the number wall. (3%)

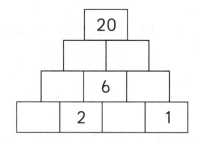

8 Do addition and subtraction using the number lines. (4%)

(a)

□○□=□

(b)

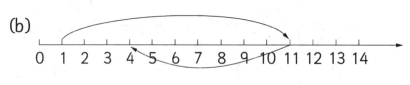

□○□○□=□

9 Choose 3 numbers from 2, 5, 7, 9 and 12 and then make two addition sentences and two subtraction sentences. (8%)

Choice 1: □□□   Choice 2: □□□

_____   _____

_____   _____

_____   _____

_____   _____

10 Fill in the brackets. (20%)

(a) 73 is made up of (   ) ones and (   ) tens. 10 tens are
(   ).

(b) Write 42 in words (   ). The tens nearest to 56 is (   ).

(c) Adding up one £5 note, two £2 coins and two 50p coins,
there are (   ) pounds in total.

(d) Fill in with suitable units of length or money.
I took 10 (   ) to buy a ruler and a 15 (   ) long pencil
in a supermarket. The cost of the ruler is 1 (   ) and the
cost of the pencil is 50 (   ).

(e) In a two-digit number, the digit in its ones place is less than
1 and the digit in its tens place is greater than 8. The
number is (   ).

(f) The "1" in the hundreds place is (   ) greater than the "1"
in the tens place.

(g) Look at the pictures and then fill in the (   ) with the
length of each shape.

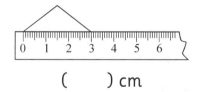
(   ) cm

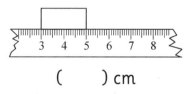
(   ) cm

(h) Write the time on the clock faces in words.

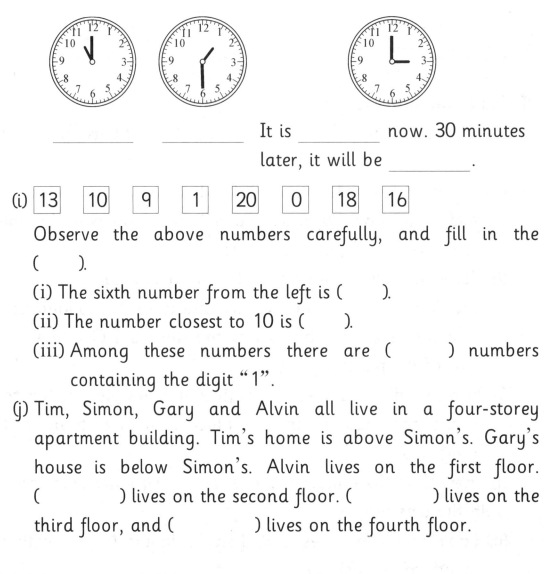

It is _____ now. 30 minutes later, it will be _____ .

(i) 13 10 9 1 20 0 18 16

Observe the above numbers carefully, and fill in the ( ).

(i) The sixth number from the left is ( ).

(ii) The number closest to 10 is ( ).

(iii) Among these numbers there are ( ) numbers containing the digit "1".

(j) Tim, Simon, Gary and Alvin all live in a four-storey apartment building. Tim's home is above Simon's. Gary's house is below Simon's. Alvin lives on the first floor. ( ) lives on the second floor. ( ) lives on the third floor, and ( ) lives on the fourth floor.

11 Make a guess. (2%)

The teacher is in the middle. There are ( ) people in the queue.

12 Read the clues to find the correct object. Write the letter of each object in the brackets. (6%)

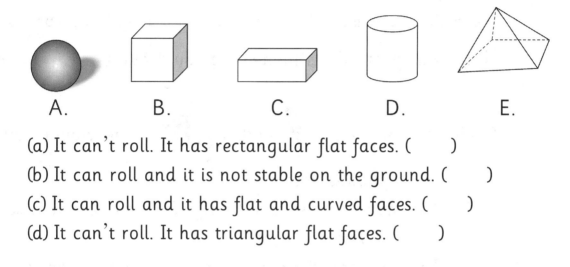

A.　　B.　　C.　　D.　　E.

(a) It can't roll. It has rectangular flat faces. (　　)

(b) It can roll and it is not stable on the ground. (　　)

(c) It can roll and it has flat and curved faces. (　　)

(d) It can't roll. It has triangular flat faces. (　　)

13 Work out the sums. (20%)

(a)

Two arrived

_____

(b)

How many are inside?

There are 16 books in total.

_____

(c)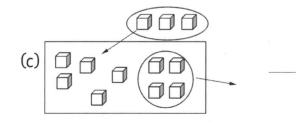

_____

(d) Tom went shopping with 20 pounds.

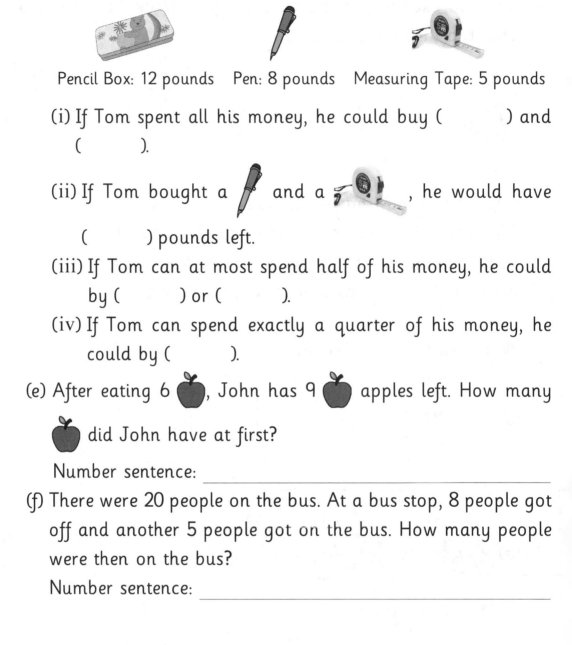

Pencil Box: 12 pounds   Pen: 8 pounds   Measuring Tape: 5 pounds

(i) If Tom spent all his money, he could buy (   ) and

(   ).

(ii) If Tom bought a [pen] and a [measuring tape], he would have

(   ) pounds left.

(iii) If Tom can at most spend half of his money, he could

by (   ) or (   ).

(iv) If Tom can spend exactly a quarter of his money, he

could by (   ).

(e) After eating 6 [apple], John has 9 [apple] apples left. How many

[apple] did John have at first?

Number sentence: _____

(f) There were 20 people on the bus. At a bus stop, 8 people got

off and another 5 people got on the bus. How many people

were then on the bus?

Number sentence: _____

Answers

Chapter 1   Numbers up to 10

1.1   Let's begin

① lines drawn from bird to tree, flower to vase, shirt to shorts, pencil to pencil box, cat to mouse   ② lines drawn from 5 butterflies to 5 triangles, 8 apples to 8 circles, 3 books to 3 hearts, 6 cars to 6 squares   ③ 1 7 4 6 3 9 2 8 10 5   ④ Black White Grey

1.2   Let's sort (1)

① Toys: helicopter, doll, cube, bear, car, football. Stationery: ring binder, laptop, pencil box, pencils, eraser, books
② On the land: grass, flowers, rabbit, tree   In the sky: bee, butterfly, bird   In the water: tadpoles, frog   ③ carrots vase   bike   cylinder   ④ In the air: 2, 4, 6   On the ground: 1, 3, 7, 8   In the water: 5, 9, 10   Animals: 1, 4, 5, 8, 9   Non-animals: 2, 3, 6, 7, 10 (answers may vary)

1.3   Let's sort (2)

① (a) Sort by size   (b) Sort by colour (c) Sort by type   (d) Sort by status (e) Sort by gender   (f) Sort by shape (g) Sort by type   (h) Sort by status
② (a) May sort by gender, by age or by height   (b) May sort by shape, colour or size.   ③ (a) Circle A: puppy, tiger, squirrel, horse, and panda   (b) Circle B: squirrel, snake and panda   (c) In both Circle A and Circle B: squirrel and panda

1.4   Let's count (1)

① lines drawn from apples and strawberries to 5, pineapples and oranges to 2, melon to 1, bananas to 4, peaches to 3, cats to 6, pandas to 8, butterflies and birds to 10, snakes to 7, squirrels to 9
② Colour 10 circles, 9 squares

1.5   Let's count (2)

① lines drawn from footballs to 3, rugby ball to 1, baseballs to 4, shuttlecocks to 5, tennis balls to 4, basketballs to 2, beach balls to 5, stripy balls to 3; table to match. batteries to 8, scissors to 10, pencil boxes to 6, flags to 7, pens to 9; table to match   ② 2   3   1   4

1.6   Let's count (3)

① A: ①   B: ②, ③, ④   C: ⑤, ⑥ D: ⑦, ⑧   ② (a) 6 3, 2 3 4 (b) 6 6 3 3, 2 2 6 8 (c) 2 6 5, 3 3 2 4 1   ③ ①, ③

1.7   Let's count (4)

① 5   8   10   9   5   6   ② 6, 7, 8, 9, 10 dots are coloured in the appropriate boxes   ③ 10 10 10   ④ answers may vary   ⑤ 10

1.8   Let's count (5)

① (a) 3 2 1 0 (b) 6 4 0
② 5 9 8 0 3   ③ 10 triangles, blank, 7 triangles, 4 triangles
④ Starting point   ⑤ 0 5 10

1.9 Let's count (6)

1 5 3, 2 4, 5 4, 1 4, 5 5, 6 1 **2** 5 white, 2 shaded 3 white, 3 shaded 2 white, 4 shaded 1 white, 5 shaded **3** 7 grey 4 black 4 grey 2 black 7 grey 4 black **4** answers may vary **5** 4 4, 10 5 5

1.10 Counting and ordering numbers (1)

1 5 first fourth **2** (a) 10 tenth fourth first seventh (b) sixth second 7 3 3 2 **3** five hearts are coloured; the fifth heart is coloured **4** (a) 3 (b) 2

1.11 Counting and ordering numbers (2)

1 10 4th coloured yellow, and the final 4 coloured yellow 5 **2** third fourth second sixth fifth **3** fifth sixth second first fourth third **4** shapes drawn in the table as described **5** second fourth third

1.12 Let's compare (1)

1 (a) tigers (b) shorts **2** (a) strawberries (b) triangles **3** 1 1, 3 7 4 4 **4** Draw 4 ○ in the first line. Draw 7△ in the second line. Draw 2 □ in the third line **5** pencil No. 2

1.13 Let's compare (2)

1 > = < **2** 4 = 4 3 < 5 4 > 2 **3** answers may vary **4** < > > = > < = < **5** answers may vary **6** the third glass

1.14 The number line

1 (b) √ (d) √ **2** (a) 2 3 4 5 6 7 9 (b) 0 4 6 10 **3** (a) 3 2 6 (b) 2 4 2 8 4 **4** (a) numbers 7, 0, 3, 2 and 9 are circled on the number line (b) 0 2 3 7 9 (c) 10 8 6 5 1 **5** 0~5 0~7 1~9 4~8

Unit test 1

1 lines drawn between pencil box and rucksack, scarf and gloves, monkey and bananas, cake and present **2** lines drawn between strawberries and seven, bananas and three, apples and 10 dots, cherries and 4, oranges and 5 dots **3** Sort by shape or size Sort by type, colour or size **4** third fifth sixth seventh 7 **5** Apples are coloured as described **6** 5 3 second fourth 2 **7** third second first fourth **8** 0 2 3 4 6 7 9 10 **9** (a) 1 3 5 7 9 1 2 9 (b) 9 3 0 **10** □ 3 ○ △ (or △ ○) **11** < > = > > 8 answers may vary for remaining questions **12** (a) 2 < 4 < 5 < 8 < 9 < 10 (b) 10 > 7 > 6 > 4 > 1 > 0

Chapter 2 Addition and subtraction within 10

2.1 Number bonds

1 1 3, 2 2, 3 1, 4 0, 1 4, 2 3, 3 2, 4 1, 5 0 **2** 3 5 5 answers may vary **3** 3 7 6 3 5 5 7 0 2 **4** (a) 3 + 3 = 2 + 4 =

1+5 (b) 7＋3＝6＋4＝5＋5＝
4＋6＝3＋7＝2＋8＝1＋9＝0＋10＝
10＋0

2.2 Addition (1)

1 8 9 5 10 10 **2** 3＋2＝5
2＋3＝5 6＋4＝10 4＋6＝10
2＋6＝8 6＋2＝8 5＋4＝9
4＋5＝9 1＋7＝8 7＋1＝8
3 10 6 8 10 6 8 10 7 3
10 **4** 1＋3＝2＋2, 1＋1＝0＋2,
4＋3＝5＋2, 3＋5＝8＋0, 5＋2＝1＋6
5 0＋5 1＋4 2＋3 3＋2
4＋1 5＋0

2.3 Addition (2)

1 (a)0＋8＝8 1＋7＝8 2＋6＝8
3＋5＝8 4＋4＝8 5＋3＝8
6＋2＝8 7＋1＝8 8＋0＝8
(b) answers may vary **2** 7 5＋5＝10
1＋7＝8 6＋4＝10 **3** 8 10 7
4 8 6 4 8 10 6 9 9
4 answers may vary

2.4 Addition (3)

1 6＋4＝10 4＋4＝8
6＋3＝9 3＋5＝8 3＋7＝10
2 (a) 3 8 6 9 7 5 1 3 ＋3
＋6 ＋0（or －0） (b) ＋4 －4 －5
＋5 3 ＋3 **3** 8 8 8 5 8 9
8 5 10 10 6 4 10 9 8 6
4 (a) 6 2 (b) 6

2.5 Let's talk and calculate (I)

1 6＋3＝9 3＋4＝7 5＋2＝7
4＋5＝9 3＋6＝9 4＋2＝6
4＋5＝9 5＋4＝9 3＋6＝9
6＋3＝9 **2** 7 6 8 8 9 10
10 7 10 7 6 1 3 5 9

3 5 9 5 8 4 10 6 9 6 7
9 7 10 7 9 10 **4** answers may
vary

2.6 Subtraction (1)

1 6－2＝4 5－3＝2 6－4＝2
7－2＝5 7－3＝4 9－3＝6
10－7＝3 **2** 4 1 2 0 1 3
5 5 5 1 2 2 0 2 3 3
3 6 6 2 8 0 6 0 1 1 2
4 5－0＝5 6－1＝5 7－2＝5
8－3＝5 9－4＝5 10－5＝5

2.7 Subtraction (2)

1 4 2 3 8 **2** 7－4＝3
10－6＝4 8－5＝3 10－3＝7
9－7＝2 7－2＝5 **3** 3 1 2
8 1 8 3 0 5 －4 －3 －6
4 4 0 5 5 1 5 3 1 3 4
3 5 8 1 0 2 **5** 4－2＝
5－3＝6－4＝7－5＝8－6＝
9－7＝10－8

2.8 Subtraction (3)

1 7－1＝6 9－5＝4 8－3＝5
9－3＝6 7－4＝3 8－5＝3
10－5＝5 6－6＝0 **2** 4 5 3
3 4 6 7 3 10 **3** 3 6 0 6
3 1 3 5 7 3 1 3
4 6＋4＝10 6－4＝2 6－4＝2

2.9 Let's talk and calculate (II)

1 6－2＝4 10－7＝3
8－5＝3 7－4＝3 9－4＝5
7－5＝2 **2** 4 4 2 3 3 1 7
1 4 2 9 4 8 1 0 **3** 3 9
0 4 10 6 7 7 9 3 1 1 3
10 4 2 **4** 4 6 9 2

2.10 Addition and subtraction

1 5+2=7 7−2=5 6+3=9
9−3=6 10−3=7 7+3=10
2 8 9 6 4 9 9 10 answers
may vary **3** 5 5 10 1 3 6 4
2 4 9 10 7 answers may vary
4 5 9,7 2,10 5,3 6,10 4,0
10 **5** 3−0 4−1 5−2 6−3
7−4 8−5 9−6 10−7

2.11 Addition and subtraction using a number line

1 0 2 4 5 6 7 8 10,1 3
5 7 9 **2** 4 3+4 = 7, 9
0+9=9,6 8−6=2 **3** 8 6 6
9 4 10 10 2 9 10 10 7 5
0 2 4 **4** 4 8 4 3 0 9 4
9 2 **5** 6 1

2.12 Games of number 10

1 lines drawn between 1 and 9, 2 and
8, 3 and 7, 4 and 6, 5 and 5, 0 and 10
2 9 8 5 5 7 4 **3** 2 4 9
7 5 **4** lines drawn between 2+8
and 3+7, 2+6 and 5+3, 9−2 and
3+4, 7−5 and 6−4, 9−3 and 8−2,
8−4 and 9−5, 6−3 and 7−4 **5** 5
10 1 9 7 8 3 10 2 4 4
answers may vary **6** > > >
< = < = < =
7 answers may vary

2.13 Adding three numbers

1 2+3+2 = 7 3+4+2 = 9
3+5+2 = 10 4+1+3=8 **2** 3
4 1+3+4=8 2 7 0+2+7=
9 **3** 7 7 10 7 5 9 9
10 10 7 10 10 **4** (a)3+2+5= 10

(b)4+2+2=8 **5** 5 4,4 3,6
2, 4 1 (First think of the number in the
box under the sentence and then the
number in the sentence)

2.14 Subtracting three numbers

1 10−2−4 = 4 10−5−3 = 2
2 2 5 9−5−2 = 2,3 1
7−1−3 = 3 **3** 1 0 2 2 4
1 0 3 0 4 2 2 2 0 0
4 (a)9−5−2 = 2 (b)9−3−4 = 2
5 5 3,9 1,3 6,8 9

2.15 Mixed addition and subtraction

1 9−4+1 = 6 9−3+4 = 10
5−1+3 = 7 9−5+2 = 6 **2** 7
4 2+7−4 = 5 3 6 10−6+3 = 7
3 < = = > > = **4** 9
7 6 10 3 2 1 9 6 8 10 7
5 8 1,7 9,8 5,0 1

Unit test 2

1 6 5 3 0 0 9 3 10 10
2 7 5 **2** lines drawn between
3+4 and 1+6, 2+2 and 8−4, 10−1
and 9−0 **3** (a) +6 2+6=8
(b) −6 7−6 = 1 (c) +5 −2
3+5−2=6 **4** lines drawn between
10 and 2+5+3 4+6−0 7−4+7, 6
and 10−1−3 9−5+2, 5 and 5+5−5
9−2−2 8−3+0 **5** 4+2 = 6
9−5=4 3+4+3 = 10 8−4−2=2

Chapter 3 Numbers up to 20 and their addition and subtraction

3.1 Numbers 11−20

1 113 12 16 14 19 11 18

15 20 **2** 11 12 14 15 16
18 20, 14 15 16, answers may vary
3 12 10 8, 10 5, 15 13 11 7
5 3 1 **4** (a) green line from 11, 13,
15, 17 and 19; red line from 20, 18, 16,
14, 12 and 10 (b) Odd numbers: 11, 13,
15, 17, 19, Even numbers: 20, 18, 16, 14,
12, 10

3.2 Tens and ones
1 14 15 11 **2** 3 16 10+6
18 10+8 20 10+10 17 10+7
3 12 − 2 = 10 10 + 5 = 15
10 + 10 = 20 16−6 = 10 **4** 12
15 19 12 15 19 8 6 3 10
10 10 **5** 4 7 10 10 10 10
2 6

3.3 Ordering numbers up to 20
1 3 4 6 8 9 12 14 15 17
19 20, 1 4 5 6 9 10 12 14
15 16 17 20 **2** colour odd numbers,
even numbers, every 5 numbers
3 (a) 14 16 (b) 19 10 (c) 12
(d) 13 14 15 16 17 (e) 16 17
18 19 **4** (b) 20 19 18 17 16
15 (c) 3 4 5 6 7 (d) 4 8 12
16 20 **5** (b) 9 (c) 18 (d) 13
6 (a) 13 or 14 (b) 17 or 18 or 19
(c) answers may vary

3.4 Addition and subtraction (I)
1 2+6 = 8 12+6 = 18 8−6 = 2
18−6 = 12 10+7 = 17 19−8 = 11
12+6 = 18 17−4 = 13 **2** 8 8
8 7 18 18 18 17 6 9 6 6
16 19 16 16 **3** 4 2 1 3
14 12 11 13 4 2 5 5 14

12 15 15 **4** 8 8 9 18
15+3 = 18 12+7 = 19 2 1 5
12 16−5 = 11 17−2 = 15 **5** =
< > < > = < = <
> > =

3.5 Addition and subtraction (II) (1)
1 14 12 12 **2** 15 14 **3** 1
2 12, 2 3 13, 4 5 15, 2 2 12,
1 8 18, 3 6 16 **4** 13 10 13,
13 10 13, 14 10 14, 14
9+1 = 10 10+4 = 14 **5** 7+8 = 15
8+7 = 15 6+9 = 15 9+6 = 15

3.6 Addition and subtraction (II) (2)
1 6+9 = 15 9+6 = 15, 8+5 = 13
5+8 = 13, 4+7 = 11 7+4 = 11,
3+10 = 13 10+3 = 13, 7+4 = 11,
3+9 = 12 **2** 13 13 12 17
11 11 **3** 11 11 12 13 12
12 13 11 13 13 14 12 14
14 15 11 15 15 16 14 16
16 11 19 17 17 12 18 18
11 13 20 **4** > < = >
> = > > < = =
5 10 15 14 12 12 17 12 16

3.7 Addition and subtraction (II) (3)
1 8 8 7 7 **2** 7 5 **3** 2 1
9, 1 5 5, 3 2 8, 6 2 8, 7 2 8,
4 2 8 **4** 9 10 9, 3 10 3, 8
10 8, 2 10 8 2 **5**

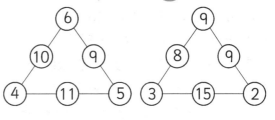

3.8 Addition and subtraction (Ⅱ) (4)

1 8 15 − 7 = 8 14 − 8 = 6
17 − 9 = 8 13 − 4 = 9 12 − 3 = 9
16 − 9 = 7 20 − 9 = 11 **2** 6 9
8 8 3 8 **3** 9 3 7 5 9 8
8 7 9 6 8 7 9 7 4 5
4 < < = > > > >
> **5** answers may vary

3.9 Addition and subtraction (Ⅱ) (5)

1 7 + 5 = 12 11 − 3 = 8
13 − 4 = 9 4 + 8 = 12 9 + 2 = 11
9 + 4 = 13 14 − 8 = 6 12 − 5 = 7
2 12 12 7 8 15 8 14 8
13 7 5 20 **3** greater than 10:
5 + 7 7 + 13 9 + 2 16 − 5 8 + 4,
less than 10: 15 − 6 13 − 8 18 − 14
4 7 12 9 13 15 17 13 8
5 **5** 3 + 9 = 4 + 8 = 5 + 7 or 4 + 9 =
5 + 8 = 6 + 7 or 3 + 8 = 4 + 7 = 5 + 6

3.10 Let's talk and calculate (Ⅲ)

1 16 − 7 = 9 12 − 9 = 3 6 + 5 = 11
9 + 7 = 16 14 − 6 = 8 7 + 5 = 12
2 (a) 6 + 7 = 13 (b) 6 + 6 − 12
(c) 12 − 3 = 9 (d) 7 + 9 = 16
(e) 12 − 8 = 4 (f) 6 + 9 = 15
3 answers may vary

3.11 Adding on and taking away

1 15 6, 9 + 7 = 16 16 − 7 = 9,
8 + 5 = 13 13 − 5 = 8 **2** 5 + 8 = 13
13 − 8 = 5, 9 + 7 = 16 16 − 7 = 9
3 18, 19 2, + 9, 19 − 5, + 1 − 1,
+ 8 − 8, 12, 12 − 5 **4** 18, 10
14, 9, 16, 10, 9 18, 11, 8, 9, 7 4 (or 4
7), 8 16, 4 9 13 **5** answers may
vary

3.12 Number walls

1
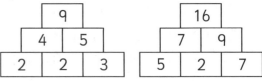
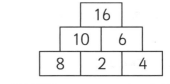
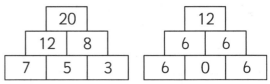
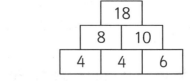
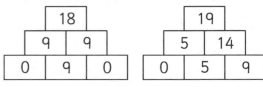

(answers may vary)

2
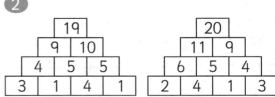
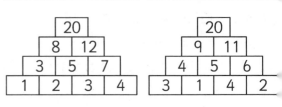
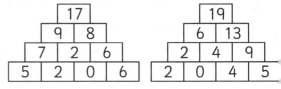

3 answers may vary

Unit test 3

①　(a) 5　10　11　14　16　18　(b) 8
12　14　13　9　7　(c) 7　10　15　9
7　②　(a) 12　17　10　8　9　18　20
10　(b)

```
      ┌─────────┐                    ┌─────────┐
      │   15    │                    │   18    │
   ┌────┬────┐                    ┌────┬────┐
   │ 8  │ 7  │                    │ 9  │ 9  │
 ┌────┬────┬────┐              ┌────┬────┬────┐
 │ 4  │ 4  │ 3  │              │ 7  │ 2  │ 7  │
 └────┴────┴────┘              └────┴────┴────┘
```

(c) lines drawn between 8: 15−7　13−5
17−9, 10: 6+4　14−4, 16: 8+8
10+6　③　7+6 = 13　13−6 = 7
4+8 = 12　12−8 = 4　16−7 = 9
11+2 = 13　④　8　9

Chapter 4　Recognising shapes

4.1　Shapes of objects (1)

①　lines drawn between matching shapes
②　4　2　4　3　2　③

	Can't roll	Can roll	
		in one direction	in all directions
🔋		✓	
📱	✓		
🏐			✓

④　1　8　2　1,0　2　4　2

4.2　Shapes of objects (2)

①　lines drawn between matching shapes
②　5　3　3　1　③　lines drawn

between matching shapes　④　7　5
10　18　⑤ 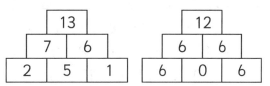　(answer may vary)

Unit test 4

①　7　10　8　4　6　12　14　11　6
10　17　8　17　17　18　12　4　12
14　answer may vary　②　5　3　2
2　3　10　5+3+2 = 10　③　3　2
1　3　2　④

```
      ┌─────────┐              ┌─────────┐
      │   13    │              │   12    │
   ┌────┬────┐              ┌────┬────┐
   │ 7  │ 6  │              │ 6  │ 6  │
 ┌────┬────┬────┐        ┌────┬────┬────┐
 │ 2  │ 5  │ 1  │        │ 6  │ 0  │ 6  │
 └────┴────┴────┘        └────┴────┴────┘
```

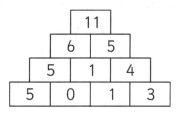

```
         ┌─────────┐
         │   11    │
      ┌────┬────┐
      │ 6  │ 5  │
   ┌────┬────┬────┐
   │ 5  │ 1  │ 4  │
 ┌────┬────┬────┬────┐
 │ 5  │ 0  │ 1  │ 3  │
 └────┴────┴────┴────┘
```

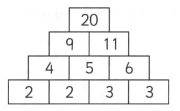

```
         ┌─────────┐
         │   20    │
      ┌────┬────┐
      │ 9  │ 11 │
   ┌────┬────┬────┐
   │ 4  │ 5  │ 6  │
 ┌────┬────┬────┬────┐
 │ 2  │ 2  │ 3  │ 3  │
 └────┴────┴────┴────┘
```

⑤　(a) ②　③　(b) ⑤　(c) ③　⑥
(d) ④　⑦　⑧　⑥　9+6 = 15
15−6 = 9 or 15−9 = 6　4+8 = 12
12−4 = 8 or 12−8 = 4　⑦　(a) 9
(b) 4

Chapter 5　Consolidation and enhancement

5.1　Sorting shapes

①　(a) 6　5　5　7　(b) 11　12
②　(a) shape　1　6　7　10　13　16,
3　5　12　15　18, 4　8　14　17, 2

9   11   (b) size   1   2   3   7   8   13
14   15, 4   5   6   9   10   11   12   16
17   (or colour   1   2   5   6   12   14
16   18, 3   7   10   13   15   17, 4   8
9   11)   **3** 0   1   2   7, 0   1   3   8,
0   1, 8

5.2   Calculating with reasoning

1 12   13   6   14   4   13   5   8   6
8   5   8   14   6   8   **2** 16   17   18
19   20, 17   16   15   7   14   6   13,
12   13   14   7   15   8   16, 12   11
10   9   8   5   6   7   14   8   15   9, 6
7   8, 6   9   5   10   **3** 12   18   12
13   19   14   14   20   16   10   9   6
9   8   6   8   7   6   **4** 7, 2, 17, 12,
2   27, 6   22, 2   37, 6   32
5 $\triangle = 5$ $\square = 6$ $\odot = 7$
$\heartsuit = 2$ $\bigcirc = 8$

5.3   Comparing numbers

1 (a) Draw 5 $\square$ (b) Draw 4 $\square$
(c) Draw 3 $\square$ (d)   Draw 6 $\triangle$
(e) Draw 3 $\bigcirc$ **2** (a) $<$ $>$ $<$ $>$
$>$ $>$ (b) $<$ $>$ $=$ $>$ $<$ $>$
(c) $<$ $<$ $<$ $=$ $=$ $>$
3 answers may vary   **4** $<$ $>$
$=$ $>$ $>$ $=$ **5** 7   8   3   10
5   7

5.4   Half and quarter

1 $\checkmark$ $\times$ $\times$ $\times$ $\checkmark$ **2** half
quarter   quarter   quarter   **3** answers
may vary   **4** answers may vary
$6 = 3 + 3$ $14 = 7 + 7$ $10 = 5 + 5$
5 18   3   10   20   4   16   6   3
6 5   9   7   **7** 10   **8** 10   5   5

5.5   Let's do additions together

1 missing additions in sequence
2 sums totaling 4, 7, 10, 13, 16 are
coloured   **3** From top to bottom: $8+$
7   $9+8$ $7+8$ $8+9, 4+7$ $5+8$
$3+8$ $4+9$ **4** $6+7$ $7+6$ $8+5$
$9+4$ $10+3, 9+9$ $10+8$ $11+7$
$12+6$ $13+5$ $14+4$ $15+3,$
$1+9$ $2+8$ $3+7$ $4+6$ $5+5$
$6+4$ $7+3$, answers may vary
5 (a) How many birds are there in the
tree now? (answer may vary) $10+8 = 18$
(b) How many children are there in the
choir altogether? (answer may vary)
$12 + 8 = 20$ (c) How many cars were
there at first? (answer may vary)
$9+6 = 15$ **6** $1+8+7$ $2+8+6$
$3+8+5$ $4+8+4$

5.6   Let's do subtractions together

1 missing subtractions in sequence
2 sums totaling 0, 3, 6, 9 are coloured
3 From top to bottom: $7-3$ $9-4$
$7-4$ $9-5, 11-3$ $13-4$ $11-4$
$13-5$ **4** $16-4$ $17-5$ $18-6$
$19-7$ $20-8, 11-3$ $12-4$ $13-5$
$14 - 6$ $15 - 7$ $16 - 8$ $17 - 9,$
$19-9$ $18-8$ $17-7$ $16-6$ $15-5$
$14 - 4$ $13 - 3, 11 - 6$ $12 - 7$
$13-8$ $14-9$ $15 - 10$ $16 - 11$
$17 - 12$ **5**   (a) How many apples
were left over? (answer may vary)
$20-8 = 12$ (b) How many rabbits are
black? (answer may vary) $15-8 = 7$
(c) How many more basketballs than
volleyballs are there in the sports room?

(Answer may vary) $12-9=3$

6 $12-11=10-9=8-7=6-5$ or

$12-10=11-9=8-6=7-5$ or

$12-8=11-7=10-6=9-5$

5.7   Making number sentences

1 $5+3=8$ $3+5=8$ $8-3=5$

$8-5=3, 4+2=6$ $2+4=6$

$6-2=4$ $6-4=2$ **2** 15

$6+9=15$ $15-9=6$ $15-6=9$,

20   $8+12=20$ $20-8=12$

$20-12=8, 7$ $9+7=16$ $7+9=16$

$16-7=9, 14$ $6+14=20$

$14+6=20$ $20-14=6$ **3** $7+8=15$

$8+7=15$ $15-7=8$ $15-8=7$,

$5+15=20$ $15+5=20$ $20-5=15$

$20-15=5, 9+0=9$ $0+9=9$

$9-0=9$ $9-9=0$ **4** $4+8=12$

$8+4=12$ $12-4=8$ $12-8=4$,

$5+9=14$ $9+5=14$ $14-9=5$

$14-5=9$ **5** $2+10=12$ $10+2=12$

$12-2=10$ $12-10=2, 6+8=14$

$8+6=14$ $14-8=6$ $14-6=8$,

$7+9=16$ $9+7=16$ $16-7=9$

$16-9=7$

5.8   Mathematics playground (1)

1 8   3   10   15   9   2   15   12

15   10   5   6   14   9   17   15   0   9

18   18   **2** (a) 9   10   11   13   14

16   17   18   19   20, 0   6   8   12

16   18   20, 15   13   11   9   5   3   1

(b) 16   20   1   8   4   (c) 2   7   5   3

3   5   (d) 7   9   13   18   20

3 (a) $7+5=12$ $5+7=12$

$12-7=5$ $12-5=7$ (b) $6+3-2=7$

or $6-2+3=7$ (c) $10-3-2=5$ or

$10-2-3=5$ **4** $<$ $>$ $<$ $=$

$<$ $<$ $<$ $<$ $>$ $=$ $=$ $<$

5 $<$ $>$

5.9   Mathematics playground (2)

1 18   10   20   18   9   3   7   11

8   15   5   0   **2** 6   4   6   9   11

13   8   17   4   **3** $4+8=12$

$8+4=12$ $12-4=8$ $12-8=4$,

$3+10=13$ $10+3=13$ $13-3=10$

$13-10=3, 8+0=8$ $0+8=8$

$8-0=8$ $8-8=0$ **4** 6   20   9

8   5   6   7   16   **5** third   sixth

fifth   first   fourth   second   **6** 4   7,

1   6, 3   5, 2   8, 4   7, 1   6, 3   5

7 4 black beads   7 white beads

5.10   Mathematics playground (3)

1 14   15   18   17   5   12   8   7

7   16   6   7   **2** 0   4   6   8   12

14   16   **3** $0<3<5<8<10<12<$

$14<20$ **4** $10+2$ $9+3$ $8+4$,

$12+8$ $13+7$ $14+6, 16-8$

$15-7$ $14-6, 12-7$ $13-8$ $14-9$

5 (a) From bottom to top: 2   3   13

(b) From bottom to top: 6   2   7   4   9

6 $<$ $>$ $=$ $>$ answers may

vary   **7**

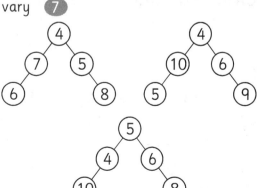

(answers may vary)

Unit test 5

1 13 9 12 6 14 11 8 8
18 0 6 7 16 5 15 15 12 9
13 20 **2** $7+5=12$ $5+7=12$
$12-5=7$ $12-7=5$ $3+9=12$
$9+3=12$ $12-3=9$ $12-9=3$,
$16-2=14$ $7-4+1=4$ or
$7+1-4=4$ **3** (a) 15 (b) 1 7
(c) 19 (d) $20>18>15>4>2>0$
4 13 14 16 17, 9 5, 8 4,
answers may vary **5** 12, 4 2, 10
5, 14 **6** 14 17 9 14 13 7 9
14 7 9 8 5 6 8 14 14 9
5 11 8 3 **7** (a) From bottom to
top: 5 4 3 9 7 16 (b) From
bottom to top: 5 2 1 3 5 8
8 $=$ $>$ $=$ $>$ answers may vary
9 From top to bottom: $5+3$ $4+3$
$5+4$ $5+5$ $3+5$; $10-4$ $12-5$
$12-6$ $10-5$ $11-6$
10 (a) $8+5=13$ (b) $15-7=8$
(c) $14-9=5$ (d) $12-7=5$
(e) $8+12=20$ (f) $15-9+10=16$
11 circle cylinder

Chapter 6 Numbers up to 100

6.1 Tens and ones

1 2 8 28 $20+8=28$, 6 5
65 $60+5=65$, 3 3 33
$30+3=33$, 8 4 84 $80+4=84$
2 2 5 25, 4 0 40 **3** 20 △,
18 △ **4** (a) 5 30 8 40 10
100 (b) 6 50 4 60 1 40 5
5 (a) 52 94 (b) 6 3 7 8
(c) tens 3 tens ones 6 ones

6.2 Knowing 100

1 30 40 50 70 80 90 100;
20 40 60 80 100 **2** 30 50
80 10 2 4 **3** 50 60 70 80
90, 40 40 40 40 40, 40 30 20
10 0, 100 90 80 70 60, 10 20
30 40 50, 50 60 70 80 90
4 40 15 28 53 **5** (a) 90 85
80 75, 8 18 28 38 (b) 89 79
69 59, 1 11 21 31

6.3 Representing numbers up to 100 (1)

1 (a) 4 6 46 (b) 5 2 52 (c) 8
0 80 **2** (b) 6 tens 8 ones (c) 5 tens
4 ones (d) 7 tens 0 ones **3** (a) 72
(b) 59 (c) 3 tens and 8 ones **4** (a) 95
61 (b) 4 7 5 2 (c) ones 4 ones
tens 8 tens

6.4 Representing numbers up to 100 (2)

1 (a) numbers 8, 26, 41, 57, 74, 88 and
92 are marked on the number line
(b) 13 27 35 49 66 71 84 98
(c) 12 14 26 28 34 36 48 50
65 67 70 72 83 85 97 99
(d) 10 20 20 30 30 40 40 50
60 70 70 80 80 90 90 100
2 72 78 70 77 79, 15 65 5
35 95, 90 93 100 81 95
3 (a) 13 23 33 43 53 63 73
83 93 (b) 60 61 62 63 64 65
66 67 68 69 (c) 50 51 52 53
54 55 56 57 58 59 (d) 55 66
77 88 99 (e) 70 **4** 13 24 35
46 57 68 79, 20 31 42 53 64

75 86 97

6.5 Comparing numbers within 100 (1)

1 numbers 18, 23, 32, 55, 68, 71 and 97 are marked on the number line

2 (a) 16 23 39 45 61 67 78 93 (b) 10 20 20 30 30 40 40 50 60 70 60 70 70 80 90 100 **3** 27 29 31 32, 60 64 66 68, 87 83 81 75 73

answers may vary **4** < < < > < > > > > < < > < < < = **5** (a) 19 < 27 < 58 < 74 < 91 < 93 (b) 6 < 46 < 60 < 76 < 86 < 96 **6** 90 47 56 71, 34 15 28 39 **7** 30 41 52 63 74 85 96 14 25 36 47 58 69

6.6 Comparing numbers within 100 (2)

1 40 60 20 5 6 8 2 3 6 9 8 **2** (a) 29 66 78 89 50 (b) 41 60 68 85 100 (c) 62 64 49 51 60 62 47 49 (d) 20 30 50 60 70 80 70 90 **3** (a) 83 87 (b) 72 90 **4** < > = > > > < < = < < > **5** (a) 99 > 88 > 86 > 66 > 27 > 17 (b) 100 > 71 > 65 > 44 > 39 > 26 **6** 18 8 78 38 88 58 28, 80 82 89 88, 80 78 82 89 88 58, 18 8 38 28

6.7 Practice and exercise (I)

1 numbers 38, 42, 59, 81, 9 and 76 are marked on the number line **2** > >

> < > < > < **3** 15 28 86 17 30 88 59 98 49 61 100 51 **4** 26 28 48 50 64 66 42 44 80 82 29 31 76 78 61 63 **5** 30 40 70 80 50 60 60 70 30 50 70 90 60 70 90 100 **6** 1 9 6 2 7 9 3 5 4 4 3 7 **7** 9 1 8 9 2 3 9 3 7 9 4 4 **8** 20 20 30 30 40 50 40 60 70 50 80 90 **9** answers may vary

6.8 Knowing money (1)

1 1 20 5 1 50 2 10 2 **2** 2 pounds 1 pound 50 pence 20 pence 10 pence 5 pence 2 pence 1 penny **3** 10 5 50 20, 50 pounds 20 pounds 10 pounds 5 pounds **4** (b) 2 (c) 5 (d) 4 (e) 5 (f) 100 **5** (a) 10 pounds (b) 5 pounds (c) 5 pounds, 2 pounds, 2 pounds, 1 pound **6** $10+5+2+1=18$ $5+5+5+2+1=18$ answers may vary

6.9 Knowing money (2)

1 (a) 75 (b) 32 60 (c) 2 90 (d) 25 23 **2** (a) 5 (b) 5 (c) 2 **3** > < > > < < **4** $10+5+5=20$ $5+5+5+2+2+1=20$ **5** (a) $20-18=2$ (pounds) (b) $15+5=120$ (pounds) (c) $8+2=10$ (pounds)

Unit test 6

1 3 7 37 $30+7=37, 5$ 3 53 $50+3=53$ **2** (a) tens 8 tens

ones   2   ones   (b) 5   50   (c) 47   (d) 8
3   (e) 92   ③ (a) 11   22   27   40   55
66   68   83   (b) 10   12   21   23   26
28   (c) 30   50   50   60   60   70
④ (a) 100   (b) 60   (c) 10   60
⑤ (a) 5   (b) 2   (c) 5
⑥ (a) 20 − 15 = 5   (b) 9 + 1 = 10
(c) answers may vary

Chapter 7   Introduction to time (I)

7.1   Year, month and day

① (a) 12   April   July   October
December   (b) 7   Monday   Thursday
Saturday   answers may vary
② Winter   Spring   Summer   Autumn
③ (a) 19 May 2016   19/05/2016
(b) No   ④ 01/01/2016   25 March 2016
Friday   25/12/2016   26 December 2016
Monday   ⑤ answers may vary

7.2   Telling the time

① (a) yesterday, today, tomorrow
(b) morning, noon, afternoon, evening
② (b) In an hour   (c) In a minute
(d) In an hour   (e) In a minute
③ (a) hours   (b) minutes   (c) hour
(d) minutes   ④ half past 10, 5 o'clock,
half past 1, 12 o'clock   ⑤ 12   12   12
⑥ answers may vary

7.3   Hour and half an hour

① half past 6   9 o'clock   11 o'clock
half past 2   ② 06:00   03:30   10:00
07:30   ③ half past 5   12 noon   1
o'clock in the afternoon   3 o'clock in the
afternoon   5 o'clock in the afternoon

half past 9 evening   ④ (a) 10 o'clock
half past 10   (b) half past 3   5 o'clock
⑤ clock faces show 4 o'clock, half past
9, half past 10, half past 7   ⑥ The
third clock.

Unit test 7

① January   April   June   August
September   December   ② Sunday
Saturday   Tuesday   Wednesday
③ 10:30   02:00   06:30   08:00   ④ 8
o'clock in the morning   half past 11   12
noon   3 o'clock in the afternoon   4
o'clock in the afternoon   half past 9 in
the evening   ⑤ 1 January 2017   01/
01/2017   14/04/2017   Friday   29 May
2017   25 December 2017   25/12/2017
26/12/2017   Tuesday   ⑥ (a) minutes
(b) hours   (c) minutes   (d) days
(e) hours   ⑦ clock faces show 7
o'clock, 5 o'clock, half past 4, half past 9
⑧ 7 o'clock   half past 7   8 o'clock
10 o'clock   half past 11   1 o'clock in
the afternoon   3 o'clock in the afternoon
half past 5 in the afternoon   6 o'clock in
the evening   half past 8 in the evening

Chapter 8   Let's practise geometry

8.1   Left and right (1)

① answers may vary   ② (a) 7
(b) (i) left   right   (ii) right   left
(c) (i) left   right   (ii) right   (d) (i) third
apple   (ii) 3   right   (iii) 5   peach
③ (a) A   B   C,   E   F   (b) right
left   (c) 3   2   (d) A   sixth

8.2 Left and right (2)

1 rose, sunflower, tulip, daffodils, daisy, orchid, plum flower **2** shapes drawn in the grid according to instructions **3** (a) 5 1 (b) 1 left 3 (c) arrows are drawn towards the carrot **4** Lines drawn from house 1 to squirrel, house 2 to frog, house 3 to Kitty and house 4 to chick

8.3 Left, centre and right, top, middle and bottom

1 second third fifth **2** (a) ④ ⑤ ⑥ (b) ① ② ③ (c) ⑦ ⑧ ⑨ (d) ⑦ ⑨ (e) ① (f) ④

3 (a)

4	9	2
3	10	5
8	1	7

(b)

4	8	2
3	5	1
10	7	6

4 (a) answers may vary (b) answer may vary (c) ○

8.4 Comparing lengths

1 right **2** giraffe rabbit **3** top middle **4** bottom middle **5** middle bottom **6** The monkey on the left

8.5 Length and height (1)

1 3rd **2** 6 9 7 **3** answers may vary **4** cm m cm m cm m

8.6 Length and height (2)

1 (a) 6 2 (b) 4 3 **2** 16 30 **3** cm m cm cm m m **4** (a) 98 − 90 = 8 (cm) (b) 80 − 8 = 72 (m)

8.7 Practice and exercise (II)

1 (a) numbers 27, 49, 85 and 92 are marked on the number line (b) 16 18 32 34 (c) 60 70 50 60 **2** (a) 7 (b) 3 2 (c) 3rd left/5th right (d) 9 8 6 5 3 2 0 **3** 3 4 5 "√" at 5 cm **4** 7 o'clock 9 o'clock half past 10 half past 11 1 o'clock in the afternoon 2 o'clock in the afternoon half past 3 in the afternoon **5** (a) 4 4 tens (b) 73 63 (c) 70 2 (d) 68 (e) 42 **6** 80 20 70 30 The ant

Unit test 8

1 (a) 6 3 9 (b) 5 8 **2** m m cm cm **3** C A **4** C **5** A

End of year test

1 7 18 8 7 1 3 10 4 20 3 **2** 38 40 **3** 10 40 60 **4** < > = answers may vary answer may vary answers may vary < < **5** 6 11 5 14 4 16 **6** From top to bottom: 5+5 6+6 6+7 **7** From bottom to top: 1 4 3 5 9 11 **8** 15 − 7 = 8 1 + 10 − 7 = 4 **9** answers may vary **10** (a) 3 7 100 (b) Forty-two 60 (c) 10 (d) pounds cm pound pence (e) 90 (f) 90 (g) 3 2 (h) 11 o'clock half past 1 3 o'clock half past 3 (i) (i) 0 (ii) 9 (iii) 5 (j) Gary Simon Tim **11** 11 **12** (a) B and C (b) A (c) D (d) E **13** (a) 3 + 2 = 5 (ducks) (b) 16 − 2 = 14 (books) (c) 9 + 3 − 4 = 8 (d) (i) a pencil box and a pen (ii) 7 (iii) a pen or a measuring tape (iv) a measuring tape (e) 6 + 9 = 15 (apples) (f) 20 − 8 + 5 = 17 (people)